COMMUNITY COLLEGES AS ECONOMIC ENGINES

The Futures Series on Community Colleges

The Futures Series on Community Colleges is designed to produce and deliver books that strike to the heart of issues that will shape the future of community colleges. Futures books examine emerging structures, systems, and business models and stretch prevailing assumptions about leadership and management by reaching beyond the limits of convention and tradition.

Topics addressed in the series are those that are vital to community colleges, but have yet to receive meaningful attention in literature, research, and analysis. Futures books are written by scholars and practitioners who deliver a unique perspective on a topic or issue—a president or higher-education consultant bringing expert and practical understanding to a topic, a policy analyst breaking down a complex problem into component parts, an academic or think tank scholar conducting incisive research, or a researcher and a practitioner working together to examine an issue through different lenses.

Futures books are developed on the premise that disruptive innovation and industry transformation are, and will be, an ongoing challenge. Gradual improvement is, understandably, a natural preference of leaders. It will not be enough, however, to position our colleges for the future. The future will be about transformation and, to perform optimally, our colleges will need to become capable of large-scale change. As leaders come face-to-face with digital forces and rapidly changing social, economic, and public policy conditions, they will have no choice but to get ahead of change or relinquish market position to competitors. Futures books are a vehicle through which leaders can learn about and prepare for what's ahead. Whether it's through analysis of what big data will mean in the next generation of colleges or which business models will become the new normal, Futures books are a resource for practitioners who realize that the ideas of out-of-the-box thinkers and the innovative practices of high performing organizations can be invaluable for answering big questions and solving complex problems.

—Richard L. Alfred, series founding editor, emeritus professor of higher education, University of Michigan; Debbie L. Sydow, series senior editor, president, Richard Bland College of the College of William and Mary; and Kate Thirolf, series editor, dean of business and human services, Jackson College

Books in The Futures Series on Community Colleges

Developing Tomorrow's Leaders: Context, Challenges, and Capabilities, by Pamela Eddy, Debbie L. Sydow, Richard L. Alfred, and Regina L. Garza Mitchell

This book provides a template for leadership development in the community college sector. The theme of the book focuses on the need to move beyond hierarchical leadership to networked leadership that taps talent throughout the institution. The transformational change required in the two-year sector demands new approaches to leading, including tolerance for risk, use of data analytics, and a focus on relationships. New and alternative means for leadership development are presented.

The Urgency of Now: Equity and Excellence, by Marcus M. Kolb, Samuel D. Cargile, et al.

The Urgency of Now asserts that in addition to being granted access to the community college, all 21st-century students need uncompromised support to succeed. Success means demonstrating relevant learning for transfer and employment and timely completion of credentials. Looking to the future, the authors contend that community colleges, both by their past successes and future challenges, are at the epicenter for determining the essential ingredients of a new student-centered system that guarantees equity and excellence.

Unrelenting Change, Innovation, and Risk: Forging the Next Generation of Community Colleges, by Daniel J. Phelan

In this book, thirty-five-year veteran Dan Phelan shares key insights from his personal and professional journey as a transformational, entrepreneurial community college leader. The book's wisdom and insights are amplified by observations gleaned from interviews and visits with dozens of leading practitioners. Drawing upon his sailing experiences, Phelan argues that leaders should stop playing it safe in the harbor because the real gains driving institutional and student success are found in uncharted waters. *Unrelenting Change, Innovation, and Risk* dares community college leaders to innovate and provides them with a tool kit for understanding changing conditions, assessing risk, and successfully navigating change.

Financing Community Colleges: Where We Are, Where We're Going, by Richard Romano and James Palmer

Grounded in an economic perspective, *Financing Community Colleges* helps college leaders make sense of the challenges they face in securing and managing the resources needed to carry out the community college mission. Finance has perpetually been an Achilles' heel for leaders at all levels of management. With the premise that leaders are better at winning battles they know something about, this book equips leaders with an understanding of the fundamentals and the complexities of community college finance. It tackles current and emerging issues with insight that is analytic and prophetic—a must-read for current and prospective leaders.

Previously published books in The Futures Series on Community Colleges

Minding the Dream: The Process and Practice of the American Community College, Second Edition, by Gail O. Mellow and Cynthia M. Heelan
First in the World: Community Colleges and America's Future, by J. Noah Brown
Community College Student Success: From Boardrooms to Classrooms, by Banessa Smith Morest
Re-visioning Community Colleges, by Debbie Sydow and Richard Alfred
Community Colleges on the Horizon: Challenge, Choice, or Abundance, by Richard Alfred, Christopher Shults, Ozan Jaquette, and Shelley Strickland

COMMUNITY COLLEGES AS ECONOMIC ENGINES

Kjell A. Christophersen

Series Founding Editor: Richard L. Alfred
Series Senior Editor: Debbie L. Sydow
Series Editor: Kate Thirolf

ROWMAN & LITTLEFIELD
Lanham • Boulder • New York • London

Published by Rowman & Littlefield
An imprint of The Rowman & Littlefield Publishing Group, Inc.
4501 Forbes Boulevard, Suite 200, Lanham, Maryland 20706
www.rowman.com

6 Tinworth Street, London SE11 5AL

Copyright © 2020 by Kjell A. Christophersen

All rights reserved. No part of this book may be reproduced in any form or by any electronic or mechanical means, including information storage and retrieval systems, without written permission from the publisher, except by a reviewer who may quote passages in a review.

British Library Cataloguing in Publication Information Available

Library of Congress Control Number: 2019950645

ISBN 9781475845877 (cloth : alk. paper)
ISBN 9781475845884 (pbk. : alk. paper)
ISBN 9781475845891 (electronic)

CONTENTS

Foreword		ix
Preface		xiii
Acknowledgments		xix
1	The Journey	1
2	The Regional Component of an Economic Impact Study	23
3	The Investment Component of an Economic Impact Study: Who Invests?	53
4	What an EIS Is Not—Dealing with the "Shortcomings": Production Possibilities Frontier	77
5	Moving the Needle: Economics and Politics	105
6	Leveraging the EIS: Program Changes	123
7	Leveraging the EIS: Nonprogram Changes	155
8	Alternative Funding Sources	175
9	Conclusions and Messages to College Presidents	189
Bibliography		199
About the Author		203

FOREWORD

Community colleges are creatures of their communities and states. While both are a great strength and source of support, they are subjected to the vagaries of public funding and economic downturns and are often easy targets when policymakers look to cut state and local budgets or shift scarce resources to other sectors deemed more politically palatable.

This was particularly true in the late 1990s, when state funding for higher education flattened, not to regain momentum until 2002. During this period, many community college leaders began pondering a better way of creating a more compelling narrative to blunt funding cuts or, better yet, convincing policymakers that the economic prowess of the sector could actually create wealth, effectively shortening the time between economic recoveries.

We approached Drs. Hank Robison and Kjell Christophersen of Emsi to ask if they believed that a better model could be created, based on their many years working on community economic development and modeling. We wanted to know if Hank and Kjell could create a new and fundamentally more robust economic impact model for community colleges.

Certainly, economic impact studies in higher education have been around for years, but none as far as we could determine reached deep into the economic fabric to mine the complexity and multiplicity of impacts—so-called economic multipliers—that presented a truer and more accurate picture of community college contributions to local and state economies.

Hank and Kjell, with initial underwriting from the ACCT trust fund, set about to design such a model. The work was challenging, and both economists confronted a learning curve about how community colleges were funded and how they made budgetary decisions amid the constant swirl of student enrollment and workforce demands. Once the fledgling model emerged, we knew it had to be tested.

With the support of Dr. Steve VanAusdle, then-president of Walla Walla Community College in Washington, the model was put through its paces, refined, tweaked, and stretched to its limits. Interesting results began to emerge, suggesting that the economic impact of Walla Walla Community College was larger and more pervasive that any of us previously imagined possible.

We at ACCT, along with Hank and Kjell, began to wonder if the results we were seeing might lend themselves to creating that elusive and powerful narrative—one that would influence policymakers to make very different choices about resource allocation in tough times. With additional work at Housatonic Community College in Connecticut, employing some creative efforts around public relations and marketing of their economic impact study further swayed the argument in favor of using economic impact models to flip the traditional funding conversation on its head. Later, economic impact studies in Minnesota led the Minnesota State Colleges and Universities Board to defy their own governor on funding cuts because of the undeniable impact those cuts would have had on the state budget relative to reducing tax receipts.

Now twenty years later, the work of Emsi, now part of the Strada Education Network, is the gold standard in economic impact modeling in higher education. Hundreds of community colleges have performed economic studies through Emsi, all of which owe their origins to the original and groundbreaking designs of the earliest model. This in turn has led to the creation of many new products to assist community colleges in improving and better targeting their resources to programs, a labor force, and occupational needs that yield high returns—both for students and taxpayers.

The results of what Hank and Kjell created have been remarkable and are often cited. The model has been scrutinized, analyzed, and disassembled countless times by skeptics and critics alike—none of whom could undermine the economic foundations and solidity of the work. I love to travel nationally and internationally and tout the incredible impact of our community colleges, and I could not do this without the economic impact model and the results it continues to yield.

While we have not yet succeeded in educating and convincing all policymakers that community colleges are legitimate engines of wealth and prosperity, we have made progress. We have been able to shift conversations away from costs to well-defined outputs that are powerful leveraging agents in the struggle to ensure that our colleges continue receive public funding and support. I will always count the economic impact model as an important contribution by ACCT. While the work is never-ending, we now have a powerful tool at our disposal as we continue to advocate for community colleges and their life-changing impact on millions of students, and on the communities where they live and work.

J. Noah Brown, president and CEO
Association of Community College Trustees

PREFACE

Back in 1999, I was on the tail end of what had been a 25-year-long career of work in international economic development for the US Agency for International Development (USAID) and the World Bank. I was preparing a report on some forestry or agricultural economics topic for a country in Africa with an editor who was also the talkative type. She was an excellent editor, and, as I recall, she was also very inquisitive about my background as an economist.

In addition to her work for my company in Washington, D.C., she also worked for the Association of Community College Trustees (ACCT), led at that time by Dr. Ray Taylor, the CEO. The ACCT office was just around the corner from my office. "Ray," she told me, "has had a vision for more than 15 years to develop a way to comprehensively measure the economic impacts of his 1,200-member colleges on the regions they serve. You should talk to him." My initial gut feeling was "What do I know about community colleges?" Literally nothing, so what would be the use? I explained that my expertise in economics was in analyzing proposed investments in natural resource management schemes in the developing world. I couldn't see myself delving into the mysteries of measuring the impact of community colleges on regional economies.

But my explanation was in vain. "It doesn't matter if you're not an expert in education economics," she insisted. "What matters is that you can apply your economics expertise to different problems, like in your report that I'm editing here, so I think you should meet with Ray." She cajoled and insisted, and, in the end, I reluctantly agreed to have her arrange a meeting.

And she did, but only after going through the same cajoling process with Ray. Each of us, as I learned later, had mentally given ourselves ten minutes to explain from each of our perspectives why we could not undertake this project now. Ray rightfully thought I was untested in higher-education economics, and I was fully occupied with other projects—so thanks but no thanks.

But then we met, and the ten minutes we had allocated to each other expanded to more than three hours. Ray explained his vision, and it was dead-on in my mind. And my always-looking-for-business and "can do" consultant mindset must have been infectious to him. I think I said something like "Well, I'm busy this week, but I think next week will be okay."

Ray's vision was vastly different from the studies that were in use back then. I knew that much. For starters, it was far more comprehensive. He thought that a study should go beyond measuring the standard regional economic impact from the college spending budgets. It should also measure the return on investment (ROI) from the perspectives of both taxpayers and students. In addition, he wanted to see the extent to which higher-education levels could be linked to lower welfare, unemployment, crime, and improved health habits. If so, these should be included as impact metrics in the form of avoided public costs.

Ray had presented this vision to think tanks, economics departments at major universities, and large consulting firms, but thus far he had found no takers. They all had similar objections to the idea. It would take too much time to develop, and therefore it would be far too costly. Some said it could not be done because of the lack of data to do proper analyses, and others said it would probably be too formulaic. And on it went.

But I had an ace up my sleeve: my Idaho-based colleague, Dr. Hank Robison—a prominent regional economist in his own right and one whose expertise, if applied to economic impact analysis, would be the perfect complement to the kind of work I was already doing in developing countries. He, too, had often worked with missing data and had overcome the problems in innovative ways. He was a "can-do" kind of economist, precisely what was needed for this kind of project. I had already tried several times to get him involved in overseas projects. His

PREFACE   xv

expertise in regional input/output modeling, along with mine on investment analysis, I surmised, would be just the ticket to come up with a comprehensive response to Ray's vision.

Ray and I agreed to take the next step, which was for Hank and me to prepare a brief concept paper on how a project like this could unfold, including the obvious caveats of running into data shortages and how to deal with them. To make a long story short, this led to a contract from ACCT to build the first iteration of a comprehensive economic impact model for community and technical colleges, which we presented at the ACCT convention in Nashville in the year 2000.

Ray's vision had now become reality in the form of an analytical model that was capable of cost-effectively measuring net regional economic impacts of community and technical colleges. Soon thereafter, we founded a new company that we aptly named CCbenefits (or community college benefits) because, after the Nashville ACCT presentation, the phone kept ringing from colleges wanting to contract with us for impact studies. Now that such studies were affordable and presumably better protected from being discredited by economists, it seemed like a huge release of a pent-up demand.

As of this writing, we have completed more than 2,000 comprehensive economic-impact studies, many of them peer-reviewed, using continually improved iterations of the model. We also changed the name of the company in 2005 to Economic Modeling Specialists International (Emsi), partly because some of the colleges were under the impression that CCbenefits was selling insurance. Dr. Noah Brown, who stepped into Ray's shoes as ACCT's CEO some five years later, continues to be very supportive. He has nurtured us along in our development as a company and we are now in our eighth year as a member of ACCT's Corporate Council.

Doing this work over the past 19 years has given us that needed credibility to author this book about what constitutes a proper economic impact study, what doesn't, and what this means for the zero-sum-game battle for funding between the education stakeholders: the K–12 system, community colleges, and universities.

The classic definition of economics as "the study of the allocation of scarce resources among alternative and competing ends" keenly applies to the nation's approximately 1,200 public community colleges. The game played by governing boards and college presidents with legislators every year is about winning their share of scarce taxpayer dollars, which is paramount in keeping the community colleges operational. Some of these colleges are now facing economic hardships, and it is only a matter of time before they have to consider shutting their doors, merging into larger community college districts, or continuing to operate while stretching their dollars—serving fewer students, using less-qualified faculty, increasing class size, and so on. Winning the public funding battle is the alpha and omega.

For many other colleges, however, the decline in public funding also signals, as it should, an emerging opportunity to rely less on state funding and more on alternative funding sources. Just because public funding is declining does not mean that colleges must curtail their operations. Embracing this opportunity means seeking increased collaboration with, and funding from, local industries, foundations, and private donors much more so than was done in the past. It is probably safe to say that the trend of declining state and public funding is not likely to reverse soon, and so the prospect of courting alternative funding sources is the new reality for community colleges.

As the colleges consider this new normal, however, they need to adjust their economic message so as to reach an audience not only of legislators, but also a broad spectrum of other stakeholders as well. They will all need to know how their financial support will economically benefit the regional economy. Local industries have specific needs for certain skills, and they will benefit from a closer alignment of programs offered at the colleges that provide those skills. This means that colleges should reach out to these industries and local firms more than they may have done in the past with specific proposals for collaboration. Foundations will benefit substantially in public relations as they spread the economic messages to the public at large. Colleges need to make their local communities more aware of how their activities increase everyone's economic well-being, not just generally, but in specific terms. Private donors will also be more prone to open their wallets if they know what their donations will do economically for the local communities.

And that's what this book is all about.

Community colleges need better economic information to continue to not only prove to legislators, but, more importantly, to prove to other stakeholders that allocating scarce resources their way will be the better economic choice. Our task at Emsi is to provide the colleges a clear assessment that the stakeholders need to make sound regional and investment decisions. For example, what portion of the regional economy can be accounted for, or explained by, the presence of a college, and why is this important to the local community? On the investment side, does it make economic sense for the taxpayers to continue funding the colleges, or should legislators rethink their decision to continue the reduction of state funding of the colleges? Does it even make economic sense for the students to attend? And finally, how do college leaders move the needle to increase the colleges' roles as economic engines?

Given Moody's bleak projections about the future of community and technical colleges,[1] this book and its exploration of the economics of community colleges is most timely. First, however, we need to do some housecleaning to make sure that the sharpened economic messaging is based on solid economic theory, will pass any peer review, and that there is no room for misinterpretation.

Improper economic impact analyses are legion, as we quickly found out when we embarked on the original project nearly two decades ago and as we run across still now. We need to know the differences between proper and improper analysis before presenting useful information and economic arguments to the legislators and other stakeholders. Obviously, colleges will want to use the information from the former and not the latter. The purpose of this book is to highlight these differences and then present the arguments for the usefulness of the impact results.

NOTE

1. Kelly Woodhouse, "Closures to Triple," *Inside Higher Ed*, September 28, 2015, https://www.insidehighered.com/news/2015/09/28/moodys-predicts-college-closures-triple-2017.

ACKNOWLEDGMENTS

None of the analyses made or stories told in this book would have seen the light of day without the involvement of some of my closest colleagues. Over the years I've had the privilege of teaming up with many of the finest professionals in the community college world. They are smart, dedicated, fun, and hardworking folks who have a love and passion for their work. My respect and admiration for them is very high. So, here's to you—my closest coworkers, and, above all, friends:

Debbie Sydow, president of Richard Bland College in Virginia. Asking me to write this book saved me from a bland retirement existence. Your most effective moment was when the unthinkable happened—I lost some files and half of my work. I was ready to quit, but you convinced me otherwise. An early adopter of the EIS while the president of Onondaga Community College, you repeated the experience several times over the years. You saw through our early mistake-prone early efforts and became a client pioneer, helping us along as we climbed the learning curve. Decades later, you became my chief editor of this book, exhibiting patience and persistence. None of this would have happened without you.

Hannah Hallock at Emsi. You held my feet to the fire on the errors I made, some fairly egregious. Your admonitions: "We don't to it that way now" gave me pause and made me realize that our modeling expertise some 20 years ago would not suffice today. It just had to be eclipsed. You and your coworkers—the next generation—did so, and with elegant and meaningful improvements. Thanks for your patient reviews of each chapter.

Tim Nadreau at Washington State University. My fellow likeminded economist and colleague, I can't think of anyone more economics-oriented than you. As a newly minted PhD, you are up-to-date on the latest economic theories and their practical relevance to the economic model we created. Thanks for being a significant part of that process over the years. And thanks for your very insightful reviews along with the pithy comments throughout—most of them incorporated.

Anna Brown, Emsi's VP of consulting services. You very much encouraged me during the early part of the writing process, and your reviews completely changed the tenor of this book. Thanks, Anna.

Hank Robison, my Emsi cofounder. We grew up together in this business and, I think, learned much from each other. You have an expertise in regional economics that is surpassed by none. I'd like to say we perfectly complement each other in our respective areas—you in regional economics, me in investment analysis—but that would be presumptuous on my part. Thanks for your reviews and suggestions.

Steve VanAusdle, president emeritus of Walla Walla Community College. As president of a pilot college for our early trial-and-error efforts at building the state-of-the-art EIS model, you taught us everything we needed to know about the community college world during the beginning stages. You taught us about the very important community college nuances we needed to incorporate into the model and about the multifaceted roles the colleges play in regional economic development. Your heart for that role was very much evidenced in how you led your college and put it on the map, not only in the region and state of Washington, but in the entire United States.

Cindy Hough, retired from the Washington State Board for Community and Technical Colleges. You have been with us from the very start. Were it not for your influence, the EIS model would not have existed, nor would Emsi. We agreed to include the social variables in the model—the impact that higher education has on lowering crime rates, improving health habits, and lowering welfare and unemployment—at your insistence. Now, in retrospect, we are very glad you won that battle. You have been our champion for as long as we have been doing this work.

ACKNOWLEDGMENTS

Noah Brown, president and CEO of ACCT. It was ACCT's brainchild to build the EIS state-of-the-art model, and you never wavered in your support of our efforts. In fact, on many occasions you provided us with the platform to serve the ACCT membership with your endorsements and blessings. You have been a true friend and supporter throughout.

Finally, the biggest thank-you goes to you, Judi, who lived through all this and tolerated all of my flaws for so long.

I

THE JOURNEY

THE BEGINNING

This chapter provides an overview of the journey of discovery reflected by the experience of Economic Modeling Specialists International (Emsi) over the past 19 years, followed by some specifics on what I believe constitutes a proper economic impact study. (Following chapters examine what a proper impact study is *not*.) For readers inclined to groan, I have made every effort to not make this into another economics textbook.

The journey began in 1999 when my cofounder and I received the contract from the Association of Community College Trustees (ACCT). Our task was to develop a state-of-the-art model to measure the economic impact that community and technical colleges had on the regions they serve.

Simple. Or so we thought.

All we had to do was to gather the data on college spending, get some gross regional product (GRP) data on the region, mix the two data sets, calculate the multiplier effect, and, voilà, we had our regional impact measure. This essentially was the sum and substance of how impact studies were done for any institution, private or public, and all we had to do was apply the same approach to higher-education institutions and dress it up with higher-education language and nuances.

Little did we know that the nuances were legion. Building a state-of-the-art model turned out to be no small task. While no model is perfect, our self-imposed golden rule was to always strive to be on the cutting edge by following best practices. We owed this to our clients, and they, in turn, needed to have a firm grasp of what they were buying. Nobody wants to allocate millions of dollars to a project, such as launching new programs at a college, only to find out after the fact that the report they used to justify the investment was deeply flawed. There is considerable political risk associated with such activity, as documented in the Reinhart and Rogoff study analyzing debt, growth, and austerity measures.[1]

We have come a long way since unveiling the first version of our college economic impact model in 2000. When we began this effort, the original scope of the project from ACCT was to:

- build a generic model that could handle the inputs from any college and analyze it in a standardized fashion;
- make that generic model as comprehensive as possible, capturing the impacts the colleges have on the regions they serve, including social metrics such as increased productivity, reduced welfare and unemployment, reduced crime, and improved health habits, all linked to education; and
- include an investment analysis component measuring the returns to state government and students resulting from the education provided by the college.

Did we successfully capture this vision? Yes, but, just as Ford's Model T captured a vision, when you compare it to the cars on the road today, it certainly wasn't perfect. When Emsi launched its first impact model, it was a Model T—state of the art at the time—and it worked well. But the results generated were certainly not nearly as well anchored in mainstream economic theory as we would have liked, and the data gaps were numerous.

In subsequent years we have rebuilt, redesigned, commissioned research to increase the accuracy and tolerances of our assumptions, and improved our methodology with up-to-date data and new literature. All of this is to say that we have been conforming to best practices and have moved the frontier of best practices forward along the way.[2]

Economic impact studies of colleges have always been a mixed bag. It is difficult, putting it mildly, to sort out the nuggets of value from studies that claim value when there isn't any. Impact studies have been around for a long time. Some are conducted by college economics faculties, some by local consultants, and some by consulting firms. Most of these contractors are assumed to be doing this work for colleges with all intentions of doing it right, but most of them are limited in their knowledge of what a true impact study is, or should be, or face limited resources in accurately measuring the true impact.

For instance, they tend to assume that doing an impact study is straightforward, i.e., it is simply a matter of taking a one-year snapshot of the college's operational spending, calculate (or quote) a multiplier, and deliver an impact measure. A long (and impressive) report detailing the methodology of input/output (I/O) analysis usually follows, after which the results of the study are publicized and the consultants move on to the next project.

And then, the college presidents and the governing boards are left to deal with the aftermath. Certainly, many studies *will* generate political reactions, some positive, but many may be, and often are, negative. Nobody likes their taxes to increase, and so people will fight, sometimes viciously, in the public square and through the media seeking to discredit the economic measures, particularly when there is a bond election in the mix. But if the results are strong, the economic impact measures are frequently used by community colleges as arguments before the legislators to secure the needed funding for the next fiscal year. Sometimes they resonate, other times they have little effect for several reasons. We will sort this all out in later chapters.

To be sure, most college presidents and governing boards naturally prefer all commentary about their colleges to be positive. If the results are only tepid, however, they will use them sparingly to stay under the political radar, particularly if they request a significant increase in funding for the next year's budget cycle. Nobody wants any catfights in the local media. Therefore, when funding is perceived to be secure and there are no looming budget cuts on the horizon or significant tax increases, impact metrics are typically used sparingly and with low-risk or friendly audiences.

On the other hand, when the money is tight and the legislature is poised to severely cut the higher-education budgets (and this is happening far more frequently now), all bets are off, and the colleges need strong ammunition to make their case to stave off the looming cuts.

Economic information is then invoked as the most effective ammunition, and many colleges widely publicize the impact metrics.

And that's where the rubber meets the road.

These impact measures had better be defensible. If not, they risk being attacked from both the political perspective and, perhaps more importantly, the economics perspective as well. In the past, the run-of-the-mill economic impact studies have not been defensible. At best, they have been questionable. If a college widely disseminates the results without the airtight assurance that they are also defensible, the president and the governing board take on an unwitting gamble when they are counting on little or no professional opposition in peer reviews. This, in turn, can feed the negative political press.

In recent years, that gamble has become increasingly costly. From the political perspective, taxpayers often feel the pressure and express their disgruntlement in op-ed pieces and letters to the editor in the local newspapers as they see their tax obligations increase. If bolstered by professional economists who discredit the results for the right reasons, the political punditry will gain credibility, and the impact study will end up detracting from, not strengthening, the college's case. While a study may be erroneous because of ignorance on the part of the consultants as to what economic theory requires, it does not absolve a president and governing board from the need to be assured that the results indeed are peer defensible.

How then do we solve this dilemma? Some presidents and governing board members are economists and could do the due diligence, but the majority of them really are at the mercy of the consultants who tell them that the results are right and credible, and so they leave themselves wide open to the onslaught of criticism without the ammunition to counteract it. Credible economic information is very powerful and, if backed up by peer support, will carry the water required to bolster the college's case when desperately needed. Erroneous economic impact information could have exactly the opposite effect.

Because they are publicly funded institutions, colleges and universities generally have a stronger need to demonstrate their stewardship of taxpayer monies before legislators.[3] For this and other reasons, economic impact studies will always be needed and will be commissioned regularly. Many impact studies, however, have received far less peer scrutiny than they should have over the past several decades, and so college presidents have become unwittingly accustomed to results that consistently overestimate benefits and underestimate costs. This, by itself, has been very difficult to undo over the years, to say the least.

The biggest challenge on this journey has been educating college presidents and governing boards that there are right and wrong ways to conduct economic impact studies. If a college had one done three years ago that showed a regional impact of $300 million, it would be rightfully upsetting if we measured an impact of only $200 million three years later. The differences couldn't be that large in just three short years, the college president claims, and questions would certainly arise.

The negative politics of it all could dominate the local news cycle, and justifiably so. Regional stakeholders and legislators would have been reminded over the past three years of the bigger impact measures, and now, with the lower numbers in hand, there would have to be some explaining. Was the model used three years ago flawed? Is the model used by us that generated the lower numbers flawed? The responsibility of correcting any errors made in previous studies would rightly fall on the institution conducting the most recent one—us. This has certainly not always been a smooth process.

THE EIS FOR COMMUNITY COLLEGES

So, we begin our discussion with the unfortunate observation that there are big differences in how practitioners conduct economic impact analyses. True, economic impact studies for colleges and universities have been conducted for decades, but many of them have blurred what exactly constitutes an economic impact. Most studies overstated the impacts, and few studies measured what we believe to be true impacts. At the same time, all of the studies used similar terminology and a similar analytical approach. But the devil is in the details, which is what we have to flesh out to gain a clear understanding of how to interpret the economic impact results and to know precisely what the results measure.

Our experience over the past 19 years has been that a college will approach us about conducting an impact study. After receiving their draft reports, they ask for clarification because their similarly sized neighbor college over in the next county had an impact study done by some other vendor with more impressive results. How can that be if our college serves just as many students and everything else is fairly similar? Or perhaps they had another firm conduct a study for them two years ago and, since then, the college has grown substantially, so how could the impact be smaller when measured this time? The answer in either case is often that the other studies were not impact studies at all, even though they might have *claimed to be*. Same terminology, similar analytic approach, different results.

Our aim here is to provide some measure of comfort for our higher-education clients who regularly contract with us for economic impact studies of their institutions. Foremost among our priorities is to promulgate a full understanding of what constitutes economic impacts—i.e., what the colleges truly added to the economic activity of the regions they serve—as opposed to other measures *billed* as impact studies, but which are not.

So, the past 19 years have given us many significant learning experiences, and we continue to learn, hopefully for as long as we are in the business of conducting economic impact studies. Several issues, discoveries, and nuances have surfaced along the way, all of which have to be addressed in one form or another, either in the model itself, or in the write-up of the results.

Cost and Continuity

One critical issue for community colleges is the cost per study. ACCT's vision was to make the impact study very affordable so the member colleges could easily and often commission one when "ammunition" from the colleges' perspective before legislative sessions was needed. The problem was that a study for one institution would typically cost up to $40,000 or more. For a four-year university, a cost of this magnitude was not particularly problematic, but for community colleges, the cost was an important issue.

To keep things simple, ACCT tasked us to reduce the cost to around $6,000 per college back in 2000,[4] a substantial drop from the average cost per study before. Furthermore, and to complicate matters, they also asked us to ensure that there would be continuity between studies conducted with the Emsi model over time—that the first year's measurements could be compared, *in a general sense*, to those derived the next time the study is conducted.

"In a general sense" is hedging in that comparing between years is tricky, since it must account for the differences in the regional and college data sets between years. Fed into the model, these different data sets will, of course, generate different results. These results can be compared, but only with the full understanding and accounting for the differences in the data. If the college grows in student headcount, therefore, it does not necessarily follow that the impacts will be greater. Intuition says it should, but the impact growth or lack thereof will depend on several different factors, some related to the college's internal data, others to differences in the economic underpinnings of the regional economy.[5]

Finally, the mandate given to us by ACCT was also to significantly reduce the workload for college institutional researchers (IRs) in charge of gathering college data. Typically, they have to spend weeks of time gathering the data, and we had to streamline the process down to two or three days.

Because of these mandates, we saw our task as one of building a model with a generic analytic capacity for all colleges, be they large, small, urban, or rural. This meant we would sacrifice some accuracy, but gain huge cost advantages. Tailored studies using highly localized data (zip codes rather than county-level data, for example) may be only marginally more precise, but they are typically very costly. We *do* capture site specificity, however, through the individual college data—the budgets, the detailed student profiles, the differences between their entry and exit levels of education, their ages, and the regions where they live.

Preparedness of the Consultants

Another conclusion we made when reviewing previous impact studies was that the consultants asked to do the impact studies for community colleges lacked the expertise in how to conduct a proper economic impact study (EIS). To use a simple analogy, one would not ask a cardiologist to perform brain surgery, though both are doctors. One cannot perform well in the specialty area of the other. Many colleges have used the wrong experts for their impact studies even though all may have been good economists generally.

Some colleges have for years used their own economics faculty to conduct an impact study because it is, by far, the least expensive way to go. Some colleges used local economic consultants, another relatively inexpensive option; and still others used reputable and large consulting firms or the economics faculty at major universities to conduct their studies, which can be much more expensive. The common denominator was that the studies are all conducted by presumably well-trained economists, but who misunderstand the metrics sought, or what they mean. Few are true experts in the area where they are asked to perform.

In order to solve this problem, we needed to become experts ourselves, which took considerable time and upfront costs on our part. In the beginning, we too misunderstood the metrics sought. Although we had some mechanical ideas on *how* to derive the measurements, they had not been part of our regular consultant repertoire, and particularly not for community colleges. I had been building economic models to analyze the investment feasibility of forestry and agricultural interventions funded by the US Agency for International Development (USAID) and the World Bank all over Africa and Asia, but had never delved into the economics of higher education. Likewise, my business partner Hank Robison had been building regional I/O models for clients interested in measuring the economic multiplier impacts of new industries entering a region or old industries leaving in terms of change in jobs, earnings, or sales, but he had never done these models for the higher-education sector.

Building a new and more comprehensive, data-driven, community college economic-impact model was new and uncharted territory for us—little did we know what we were in for as we embarked on this process. The learning curve was steep, and confirmed why ACCT's vision had not had any takers for nearly 15 years.

The prerequisite to building this new and improved model was to first understand precisely how impact studies of colleges had been conducted in the past, and from there, to identify areas to improve them. As we embarked on a literature review of past impact studies for both community colleges and universities, however, we quickly learned that most of them came up far short. The common denominator was that the regional economic impacts were being measured based on a snapshot of one year's operation of the college. It was all about the college's spending and the multiplier effect of that spending. If a college spends 80 percent of a $100 million budget in the local region and the multiplier is 2, then the regional impact would be $160 million ($100 million x 80% x 2 = $160 million). End of story.

There is nothing inherently wrong with this approach because it is not necessarily in error. But the devil is in the details, and there were a lot of missing details with such an approach. One of our main challenges was to build a state-of-the-art model that would reduce the likelihood of negative peer reviews easily derailing the intended political goodwill that the economic impact metrics were intended to generate. Given this challenge, and since words matter, we were fixated on the word "impacts," and this led to our first major discovery: the net versus gross impacts.

Net vs. Gross Impacts: An Introduction

The important details of this discovery will be discussed in chapters 2 and 3, so this is only a brief introduction. The net-versus-gross impacts distinction is the main reason why we concluded that consultants conducting the EIS for community colleges were ill prepared. None of the models we reviewed were clearly measuring true net impacts. Most of them measured gross impacts and all of them, at the very least, blurred the distinction between net and gross impacts. Net impacts are what presidents and governing boards should want to convey to the stakeholders, not gross impacts. Gross impacts, while larger and seemingly more powerful, invite discrediting from peers and plenty of negative political commentary.

One major step in our road to become EIS experts, therefore, was the improvement we made in our model to adjust for the funding structure of colleges and properly account for the "broken window" principle.[6] This ensured the reporting of only the net impacts. Absent this fundamental change, our model too would only be presenting gross impact measures, which we thought was merely "rearranging the furniture."

The "broken window" principle is as follows: Suppose an errant baseball breaks a windowpane on a hot summer night. The visible impact is a broken window that needs to be replaced. The good news is that the glazier benefits from the sale of a replacement window—a plus side for the local economy. This visible transaction has, in the analyst's mind, not only contributed positively and directly to economic growth, but also indirectly through a multiplier effect as the glazier spends his added income from the sale of the replacement window. Given this reasoning, the batter could be kindly regarded as a public benefactor, having created additional economic growth by breaking the window—the gross impact has been positive.

What's missing, of course, are the negative, but invisible impacts. We know that the biggest loser is the owner of the broken window and the biggest beneficiary is the glazier. Whereas the economy grows through the transaction with the glazier, the house owner *loses* because he now has less money to spend on other things.

And that's when the invisible impacts become real.

For example, the local tailor loses because he didn't receive an order for that new suit the house owner had wanted but now can't afford. In addition, all the other vendors who would have benefited from the money earned by the tailor if the suit had been procured are also losers because the initial money was instead spent on replacing the broken window. In reality, the net impact of the errant baseball incident is that essentially nothing is added to economic growth. While the glazier's gains are obvious, the invisible losses to the tailor and all of the vendors not benefiting from business from the tailor offset those gains.

The "broken window" principle applies to community colleges as well. The taxpayers spend money to support the colleges, just like paying the glazier to replace the broken window. The question that should come to mind right away is whether the taxpayer money could not have been spent on other things, instead of spending it on the colleges. And if so, the multiplier impact they would generate elsewhere would cancel out (plus or minus some) the impacts generated from spending the money on the colleges.

It is easy to see the political damage that the failure to account for this effect can cause for the colleges over the long run. Overinflated numbers have been publicized for years and often remain unchallenged. As we built our model, we took great care to be fully aware of and transparently account for the impacts that *would* have occurred elsewhere if the state and local funding now allocated to the colleges had instead been allocated to other sectors.

Return on Investment (ROI)

Our second major discovery was that most of the impact studies included only the regional impact component based on the college's spending, but largely ignored the return on investment (ROI) dimension from the taxpayer and student perspectives (the investment analysis component will be discussed in detail in chapter 3). Some (but not many) of the studies we reviewed did measure the investment ROI of the students and the taxpayers, although they too were fraught with what we saw as gross versus net errors. The questions in the minds of students and taxpayers are:

- Does it make economic sense for the students to attend? Are they better off with the education than without it?
- Should taxpayers continue funding the colleges? Is there a measurable return for the taxpayers?

These are appropriate questions to include in an impact study so as to gain a better measure of the value a college may have for the region it serves. In our model, we are not just looking at a measure of what the institution spends. We take into account the students' increased standard of living that is made possible through the education they receive. We also consider the increased productivity gained by the regional workforce as a result of the students' receiving the skills and knowledge of the college. Part of our task was to build the student and taxpayer investment sides into the model, and thereby confirm the strength of the regional economic impacts.

Education Impacts

A third discovery was that none of the studies we reviewed considered the *cumulative* impact from the education received by the students, not only for the analysis year, but also longitudinally. The simple fact is that the regional workforce is increasing in both quality and quantity over time as the college continuously supplies it with skilled workers.

All else being equal, students receiving education at college have more skills when they exit than when they entered. They have become more productive. That measurable gain in productivity has value in the marketplace for which employers are willing to pay more. Over time, therefore, the regional workforce gains both in quantity and quality as the college continues to supply talent. In addition, it gains even further, we assume, because the industries in the region themselves attract new companies as the reputation of the regional workforce rises. It is a benevolent circle. New companies are powerfully attracted to the promise of skilled human capital; after all, human capital is a company's most important asset.

This cumulative increased productivity measure adds substantially to the economic impact that a college can claim in the region it serves. Adding this longitudinal feature to the model provides a far more interesting and significant impact measure than what was claimed from simply the institutional spending during the analysis year.

Positive Externalities

A fourth discovery was that none of the studies we reviewed accounted for any of the positive externalities of students being educated by the college.[7] A positive externality is a "reward" enjoyed by a third party as a result of an economic transaction. The transaction is that students pay to receive an education, which the colleges supply. The third party is the public at large who reaps the benefits of a more productive economy, *plus the added benefits* of having residents who commit fewer crimes, who practice better health habits, and who tap into the unemployment and welfare services less—all because of the education they receive. These are benefits expressed as avoided costs—or costs the state does not have to incur.

This was not spectacularly difficult, we thought, although it turned out that an extensive literature review was ahead of us. The externalities identified in the scope-of-work (SOW) that we had to correlate with rising education levels included variables such as welfare and unemployment, alcohol and tobacco (health habits) abuse, and crime. Our charge was to determine if we can correlate available data with increased education levels, and if so, can we measure how much we can legitimately include in the college's investment analysis returns while not violating any fundamental economic principles? As it turned out, we found rich data that we could use to correlate improved social behaviors with higher-education levels.

WHY A COMMUNITY COLLEGE ANALYSIS MUST BE DIFFERENT

The basic structure of the model was built during the pilot phase, in which we analyzed a large urban college (EvCC—Everett Community College) and a much smaller rural college (WWCC—Walla Walla Community College), both in the state of Washington. The process was fraught with many challenges, which would have given us considerable pause in embarking on this project if we had known of them beforehand. Our naïve assumption was to build a generic model, inclusive of the improvements described above, that could work equally well for both community colleges and universities, indeed for all higher-education institutions.

But, alas, no such assumption would pan out, as we soon found out during the initial interviews with the then presidents of EvCC and WWCC, Dr. Charlie Earl and Dr. Steve VanAusdle, respectively. They told us in no uncertain terms that community colleges were different and that the model had to be tweaked in many ways to accommodate characteristics of community colleges that were far different from four-year universities.

There are differences between community colleges and universities, and they are significant. The modeling framework for community colleges must, therefore, be more vigilant in accounting for them. The unique characteristics required us to delve into some details we would never have considered were it not for the explanations provided by Dr. Earl and Dr. VanAusdle, and in no small measure, Dr. Cindy Hough, who was then at the Washington State Board for Community and Technical Colleges (SBCTC). Their explanations enriched both the development of the model and writing the reports because the differences provided context to the results. This process is still ongoing and should never stop—there will always be improvements to the model as we continuously learn from our clients.

Learning about these characteristics made our journey very worthwhile, but also very difficult. There are nuances that all community college presidents intuitively know, but they don't articulate nearly enough. With a richer appreciation for and understanding of the economic impact study metrics, however, community college leaders can turn these differences or nuances from what many in the media and political world perceive as negatives into positives. By doing so, they will succeed in putting the economic role of the community college in an entirely different light and have the data to back it up. It is in characterizing the economic impacts where these nuances can greatly enrich the dialogue with the stakeholders.

College of Choice

One of the perceived negative talking points so easily and often invoked is that a community college is there for students who cannot otherwise gain access to a four-year university. In a broad sense, community colleges do indeed provide the opportunity for many young people who cannot afford to attend a four-year university. Community colleges are considerably less expensive than universities, and many students take advantage of this flexibility, preferring to stay closer to home for their first two years of higher education before moving on to either the workforce or universities. This way, the two (or more) years spent at a community college before transferring in no way detract from the "glory" of eventually graduating from a perhaps better-known four-year university. They would still be bona fide alumnae of the university while having saved money during the first two years of their higher education.

Community colleges also offer the opportunity for young people to complete a vocational pathway—they could become plumbers, auto mechanics, welders, pipe fitters, or wind turbine technicians, etc. The opportunities abound, and the colleges are getting better each year at informing the prospective students about well-paying vocational employment opportunities in the marketplace. An added advantage is that community colleges are continually building relationships with regional businesses and industries (more so than universities do) to make the education they offer more relevant to the regional workforce demands.

The role of community colleges is much more than allowing students to complete basic courses and then transfer to universities where they eventually earn their bachelor's degrees. Academic pathways are only a small fraction of the viable options out there. In fact, the opportunities in the vocational areas are sometimes more financially rewarding and more numerous. For example, Georgetown University published a state-by-state analysis of good jobs that pay well without a BA in 2017,[8] a report well worth noting and one that community college leaders should use extensively in their marketing to parents of young impressionable students about to enter higher education.

Why are all these talking points important? First, from the model perspective, the *lower-cost tuition* means that a community college student generally invests *less* in his or her education than a student at a four-year university. And this means that the ROI for a typical community college student is generally higher than for a four-year university student, all else being equal (i.e., when comparing two years at a community college to two years at a university).

Second, a little-known fact is that community colleges in recent years are becoming just as academically rigorous as four-year universities, and colleges and universities are getting much better at reaching articulation agreements to ease the process of transferring (as in the case of between Valencia College and the University of Central Florida, for example).[9]

The messaging here should be to counter the negative talking points easily invoked by so many. Instead, it should be that community colleges should be the higher-education institutions of *choice*, not of the *last resort*. This is something to communicate far more forcefully by the college presidents to regional stakeholders as a strong argument for choosing the community college for at least two of the four years required for a bachelor's degree.

ROI Revisited

A second characteristic of community colleges is drawn from the data we have collected from the more than 2,000 economic impact studies conducted over the past 19 years—there appears to be a slightly higher ROI for community college students than for four-year university students.[10] Here is how it works. On average, and from the perspective of the students, the data consistently show that the steepest portion of the earnings curve occurs for the students served by community colleges. These students range from those who have less than a high-school diploma to those who have completed two years beyond high school, including those who earn an AA degree. Of course, the earnings still increase as students continue their education for the next two years at four-year universities, but the rate of increased earnings gradually decreases.[11] So we see that bachelor's degree holders earn more money, but it takes the students longer to get there, and the costs are much higher.

This (general) fact is largely a function of the numerous job opportunities for middle-skill workers, particularly in the vocational occupations. And that's bread and butter for community colleges. Yes, they do transfer larger numbers of students to four-year universities, but an even larger number of their students are entering the workforce each year for relatively high-wage middle-skill occupations. In general, there is a higher propensity for regional businesses to employ community college students because they, more so than university graduates, are known quantities who have acquired skills that are more relevant to the specific needs of the businesses. Because of the long-lasting relationships built over time between community colleges and regional businesses, therefore, the employers often bring the students in initially as interns and nurture them through their educational process (sometimes even through the eventual bachelor's degree).

Versatility

A third characteristic of a typical community college is that it is designed to be more open than a four-year university. By virtue of its regional and open-access mandates, the students attracted tend to be more diverse than in most four-year universities, at least in terms of their educational objectives. (There are also problematic aspects to the open-access policy, which will be discussed later.) Many students in the United States choose to enter a community college for the first two years for cost reasons before they transfer to a four-year university where they will eventually earn a bachelor's degree. Another sizable group attends to earn vocational certificates or associate degrees only. And many students attend for nonacademic reasons such as gaining certain skills in workshops or in short-term training sessions.

Noncredit Students

Probably the biggest difference between community colleges and four-year universities (and why the assumptions we make must be different as we analyze community colleges), is the noncredit students. The community colleges serve a lot of them, the universities only a few. In interviews with numerous college presidents, the opinion is that noncredit studies have an equal value to academic programs that lead to degrees, sometimes an even greater value. Community colleges tend to place as much emphasis on preparing people for jobs through noncredit activities as they do through academic education (the associates degrees and/or certificates).

Noncredit workforce training is a big part of what community colleges do, and more of them seek to accommodate regional employers who look for technical up-skilling, not necessarily degrees. As the data show, all education has value, and the value of noncredit training must be measured and accounted for in the college's impact study. Our economic model, therefore, had to be built to include students of all stripes served during the analysis year as part of the total headcount, not just those students pursuing an academic track.

And *that* was not an easy task, as it turned out.[12] Incorporating noncredit students into the model to count their impact also meant we had to differentiate between noncredit or non-degree-seeking students, and also further differentiate the latter subgroup between up-skilling (which leads to earnings increases) and merely additional training that leads to an enhanced quality of life and not to any earnings increase. Retirees interested in becoming better artists, for example, would be counted in the total headcount, but not be counted as contributors to any overall economic impact.

So, it was necessary to separate academic from non-degree-seeking students in the model. And this led to a significant side benefit, but one that most college presidents do not necessarily communicate. Colleges *can* counter the consistently negative press they receive for low graduation rates if they only included the noncredit students in their arguments. We typically see that out of a student body headcount of, say 10,000 students, perhaps as many as 3,000 to 4,000 students are workforce and noncredit students who are not on a graduation track. However, when they are included in the total unduplicated headcount, they will pull the average graduation rates down relative to the total student body. The graduation rate at a community college is, therefore, not comparable to that of a four-year university. It needs to be understood in its proper context.

Stop-Outs

The opportunity to effectively counter the negative perception that community colleges have low graduation rates is provided by another community college characteristic: the stop-outs. The 1,200 or so community and technical colleges in the United States are challenged to supply workers to industries in a very demand-driven environment. Companies need workers with skills, which community colleges supply at a reasonable cost. It has all the elements of a benevolent circle, yet one not recognized as such by some policymakers. To them, the Holy Grail is retention and the achievement of credentials. And so, if colleges graduate relatively few students with certificates and associate degrees, the perception is that they have failed in their mission and will eventually score low on the College Scorecard.

However, this begs the question of what should be a top priority for the colleges in *their* role of fostering regional economic development, apart from the Economic Development Councils (EDCs) and Workforce Development Boards (WDBs)? Without a steady supply of specific skills to the workforce, companies will soon suffer from low and sinking productivity, a certain path to a slow and gradual death. Or they get swallowed up by the competition. Or they are offshored.

On paper, companies' need for skills should ideally be met as soon as students have successfully reached the final credential—the certificate or the associate degree. This, however, is far from what happens in reality. The clear majority of vocational jobs do not require a credential, and the demand as reflected by job postings far outstrips the supply of workers. Thus, when students enter a welding program at a community college, for example, those students may be short of graduation by one full year by the time lucrative job offers begin to appear.

Enter the stop-outs phenomenon, a decades-long characteristic of community colleges that now goes against the grain of the retention and graduation objectives. Colleges have, since their inception, fulfilled one significant market niche, namely, serving the millions of "hybrid" students who have one leg in academia and the other in the workforce. Many of these are students who have families to support, attend college part-time, and who would at any moment respond to real job offers with companies not requiring the credentials. Some are already gainfully employed and have limited time to pursue their education, some are actively applying for jobs while attending, and some can only attend part-time because they have child-rearing duties, etc.

But the political reality is different. The politicians say so, with the media in lockstep. They lament that far too few community college students graduate with an associate degree or a certificate in any given year relative to the growth in jobs that require at least an associate degree or a certificate. True enough, a higher graduation rate in any given year *would be* desirable if the workforce needs were perfectly accommodating. But they are not. Skills are always in demand, and when the demand for labor is hot, workers should not be discouraged from access to well-paying jobs when they are available in the marketplace just because those workers' skills are not yet credentialed.

There are all sorts of legitimate reasons why graduation rates are low, and they are not necessarily bad reasons requiring changes in institutional priorities or behaviors. Life happens, and colleges that are supple enough to accommodate this phenomenon should be praised, not chastised. Community college students are, on average, in residence for far less than full time during the analysis year, which makes them part-time students. This merely reflects a truer picture of life and all its vicissitudes. The fact that community colleges accommodate, in many ways, people in different walks of life with widely diverse needs can just as easily be considered a blessing to local communities instead of a weakness in need of correction.

It is far better for the regional economy, we believe, to have real jobs pull semiqualified candidates away from their studies before they graduate than to not fill those critically important jobs. Many (if not most) of these students later exercise the option to return to the classroom to complete their credentials after having gained experience and, perhaps more importantly, having acquired a keener understanding and love for the work in their chosen professions. So instead of completing the certificate in one year, or the associate degree in two years, they may do so in four or six years, respectively.

This phenomenon *should not be recognized as negative; it should be regarded as positive.* It is incumbent on college leaders, therefore, to forcefully counter the negative perception about stop-outs. The fact that community colleges are a fertile recruiting ground for local companies who need employees urgently and are happy to hire away only partially skilled people before they complete their studies is certainly not a characteristic in need of changing.

But to be fair, many colleges join the political bandwagon of aggressively promoting increased retention because there is a built-in incentive to do so. Quite simply, the system provides the incentive by linking public funding to enrollment. The more students enrolled and staying in school, the higher the funding. Perhaps it would a good idea to change this incentive to one that offers public funding based on the number of gainfully employed alumni. Just sayin' . . .

CONCLUSION

It is a zero-sum game. If the legislators allocate more resources for the K–12 and university sectors, it means there will be less available for community colleges (more on this later). The community colleges are squeezed between these two other sectors of the education system in most states. In practical terms, this phenomenon is actually caused by legislators or politicians not fully understanding or appreciating the important (and sometimes desirable) nuances and characteristics of community colleges. We are uncertain as to why this is so, although our suspicion is that it might help if the negative perceptions discussed above were better articulated to policymakers by the colleges themselves as positive characteristics.

Every year has a new twist, but politicians in the end urge community colleges to behave more like universities by focusing on students achieving degrees at the cost of reducing other important services they provide but which don't fall within the purview of the more important retention objective. This certainly was reflected in the US Department of Education's College Scorecard when it was first issued in 2015, where low retention and graduation rates negatively affected community colleges' quality score compared to most four-year universities.

A community college education is not all about graduation success, or about obtaining some degree or diploma to hang on the wall. Large numbers of young and not-so-young people attend community colleges as noncredit workforce students just to receive up-skilling. Others are in remedial training programs or in dual programs (with K–12). Still others are simply continuing students—and many of them are on a slow track to earn a degree or certificate.

Our model, after having gone through several iterations over the past 19 years, currently reflects most of the community college nuances or characteristics, and the economic impact results are presented in the context of those characteristics. We succeeded in building a state-of-the-art model for community colleges that extensively uses economic data characterizing the regions served by individual colleges. These data are then merged with college-specific data to generate the economic impact measures. The model has passed numerous reviews conducted by several of our clients.

NOTES

1. Carmen Reinhart and Kenneth Rogoff, *This Time Is Different: Eight Centuries of Financial Folly* (Princeton, NJ: Princeton University Press, 2011).

2. The study period for a college is typically four months from contract signature to the electronic delivery of the final reports. Approximately one month is devoted to data collection from the individual colleges, followed by another three months to generate draft and final reports. During the data-collection time, the analyst and the college institutional research staff work closely together to ensure that the latter *and* the college president fully understand the data, how it all blends and works together, the assumptions, and what the results mean.

3. Some private institutions, it should be pointed out, buy an impact study to show the regional alumni impact and student ROI.

4. When we began the process of building the state-of-the-art model, our charge was to make it possible for a college to contract for an EIS for $6,000 per study, and still make a reasonable profit. Since then, however, the cost per college has risen to approximately $15,000 or more today because of inflationary pressures, or because colleges want something tailor-made to their college in addition to the standard EIS deliverables.

5. It becomes more complicated if different consultants are commissioned to conduct impact studies at different times. In this case, the warning signs flash, and the college leaders become responsible for ensuring that the different analysts adhere to the same fundamental rules of how to conduct economic impact studies for colleges. Ensuring continuity both reduces the cost and increases the effectiveness of the studies over time.

6. The "broken window" parable was immortalized by Frédéric Bastiat in 1850. It illustrates the importance of accounting for the opportunity cost of spending on A (the seen) when that money could also have been spent on B (the unseen).

7. It really was not a *discovery* in the true sense of the word because it was specifically required in our scope-of-work from ACCT; i.e., to include the externalities to the extent possible in our model build.

8. Anthony P. Carnevale, Jeff Strohl, and Neil Ridley, *Good Jobs That Pay without a BA: A State-by-State Analysis* , Georgetown University, Center on Education and the Workforce, McCourt School of Public Policy, 2017.

9. Education Corner, *Community Colleges vs. Universities*, 2019, https://www.educationcorner.com/community-college-vs-university.html.

10. Emsi EIS database; Grace Chen, "Studies Show Community College May Offer Superior ROI to Some Four-Year Schools," *Community College Review*, September 4, 2017, https://www. communitycollegereview.com/blog/studies-show-community-college-may-offer-superior-roi-to-some-four-year-schools.

11. Ibid.

12. Every credit hour equivalent (CHE) in the modeling framework has value. For the noncredit students taking noncredit courses, we converted the time spent in the classroom to a credit hour equivalent, or CHE. One CHE is equal to 15 contact hours in a semester system and 10 hours in a quarter system.

2

THE REGIONAL COMPONENT OF AN ECONOMIC IMPACT STUDY

SETTING THE STAGE: THE WHYS AND HOWS OF AN EIS

There are two analytical components of the Emsi economic impact study (EIS)—the first one is the regional analysis, the second is the investment analysis. Whenever impact studies of colleges are undertaken by any analyst, all of them will always include the regional spending and multiplier analysis. Far fewer, however, add the investment analysis from the student and taxpayer perspectives. Technically, the returns on the investment (ROI) made by the students and taxpayers are not part of the overall impacts claimed by the colleges; they are only included to confirm that the *colleges are spending their budgets on the right things*. If the colleges spend in areas that do not generate corresponding returns, or only tepid returns, the resulting impacts will be lower.

The best practice as of this writing is that both the regional *and* investment components should be included to ensure that the colleges receive a comprehensive picture of the economic impacts the colleges have on the regions served. In this chapter, we introduce the regional component after first setting the stage with some common-to-both elements of the EIS model. The investment analysis is introduced in chapter 3.

Public Investments

An economic impact analysis is mandatory in most states when proposed investments require taxpayer money. The purpose of an EIS is to determine if there is good economic reason to allocate taxpayer money for one-time projects such as building highways and hydroelectric dams, creating state parks, and the like. Impact analyses in these cases estimate the changes in economic activity in the region caused by the project having been completed (*ex post*), and compare those results to the economic activity that takes place without the project (*ex ante*). The changes are usually expressed as before-and-after differences in the region's gross regional product (GRP),[1] with details on which industries will be affected and by how much. In other words, were it not for the investments made in the highway, the construction of the hydroelectric dam, or the creation of the state park, the regional economy would be bigger or smaller by a certain amount.

An EIS for community colleges is not required because the colleges already exist. They are not new projects, and so the only decisions before the legislatures is whether taxpayer funding for the colleges next year should increase, stay the same, or be cut.

Economic impact studies for colleges, however, are still in high demand. State legislators may want to see economic impact numbers before voting for or against any proposed changes in the funding formulas for the colleges. And college presidents and governing boards all need "ammunition" to bolster their case for funding as they present it to the legislators. Both sides want the economic information for different reasons. This actually makes our case reasonable and (dare we say), convincing, that an EIS should be an annual occurrence, not just something the college does every three years or so.

The real shelf life of an EIS is only one year because the data characterizing the region and the college are fresh. Older data quickly becomes stale. The stakeholders move on, they retire, or they become unelected, with new actors coming on the scene. All new stakeholders need convincing, and that can only be done effectively with fresh data. All the turbulence among the stakeholders who decide for or against the taxpayer funding for the colleges each year really is a strong argument for making the EIS an annual feature.

THE REGIONAL COMPONENT OF AN ECONOMIC IMPACT STUDY 25

More recently, there has been an uptick in the interest in economic impact studies because state funding is shrinking in many states.[2] With this reality in mind, the burden on the colleges in the short term is to secure as big of a slice of this shrinking pie as possible. That burden alone is a strong reason to be able to show favorable economic impact metrics, which is *not* done with older data. The EIS is conducted with the audited and most recent data available for the analysis year.

Equally important, however, colleges are quickly learning the reality that state funding cannot be the only major source of funding in town, and they must gradually begin approaching and courting new revenue sources. (See chapter 8 for more detail on alternative sources of funding.) Economic impact metrics based on the most recent data possible will therefore continue to play a major part as colleges identify and secure alternative sources of funding.

In this context, the EIS results aren't just for legislators but can be used to approach alternative sources of funding, such as private donations and maximizing revenues from tuition. There is progress, however. Over the years, the EIS has been used not only to acquire state funding, but also to raise community support of the college. If people, beyond just the legislators, understand the value of the college, then they will be less likely to protest when the college requests funding. Public support can be a powerful tool.

A One-Year Snapshot

The standard for an EIS is based on a *one-year snapshot* of all activities of the college. That snapshot consists of two data sets: one from the region the college serves, and one from the college itself. These data sets are merged in such a way that the activities of the college are shown to generate economic impacts measured as increases in the GRP. The economic impacts are linked to the college's spending in and outside the region as calibrated to the total student headcount, demographics, and achievements during the analysis year.

For the one-year snapshot, the two data sets must be as recent as possible, typically the latest year for which the college and the region have audited data. Otherwise, the economic impact measures would not reflect the current health of the regional economy. The *college* data set includes its budget and spending patterns, sources of revenues, student headcount, the origin of their students, and their achievements. The *regional data* set includes higher earnings of the students, the GRP, and statistics on industries, occupations, and demographics. This data is used to measure the strength of the economy before and after the college has completed its activities during the analysis year.

The model essentially measures what the economy would look like with and without the college. The difference between the two is the extent to which the GRP is affected. From this one-year snapshot of data, then, we can tell whether the regional economy is better off with the college than without it, and by how much for the analysis year. This, in summary, is a measure of the added economic activities in the region attributable to the college.

Gender, Ethnicity, and Age

We express these metrics for the entire student body in attendance during the analysis year. *All* students contribute to the economic impacts with the education they receive, but those impacts differ based on demographic profiles, educational achievements, or whether they are academic or vocational. Students of all stripes, therefore, are profiled by gender, ethnicity, age, and by various levels of educational achievements during the snapshot analysis year.

The gender and ethnicity distinctions are made because the data show that average earnings before and after the education differ between males and females, as well as between ethnicities, and different age-groups. They are important input parameters because the regional and national databases clearly tell us so. We use this information, as we should, but also recognize that there is much sensitivity with it. Therefore, we do not make any gender- or ethnicity-related recommendations for the colleges, such as changing the program mix to accommodate more women, or men, because that may increase the regional economic impacts. Our purpose is merely to estimate impacts based on how the colleges actually spend their budgets, not to make recommendations.

The average age of the students also matters when measuring their earnings impact.[3] Older students have less time left to spend in the workforce than younger students.[4] Student achievements during the analysis year are measured for each student category in order to determine the average increase in credit hour equivalents (CHEs) during the analysis year to apply to the overall impact measure. The age profile used in the analysis is taken into account because we are dealing with a highly diverse student body composed of all ages, academic or vocational pursuits, and achievement levels.

It is not practically possible to do individual student analysis and aggregate them for a single college, so the use of an average is the best solution. Also, it should be noted that we do apply different adjustments to different age-groups, (i.e., students under high-school age and older students), specifically in our calculation of the adjustment for work experience and again in our calculation of student opportunity costs. We do this to account for the fact that benefits and costs differ between younger students who are coming directly from high school, and older students who have been active for a number of years in the workforce.

All of these variables are accounted for so that the overall economic impact of the current student body on the region can be accurately measured. In addition to this, we also measure the impact from the *past* students remaining in the regional workforce (see the alumni effect section below in this chapter for more detailed discussion on the past students).

Earnings

The Emsi model accounts for earnings differentials (before and after education), which allows us to measure the returns not only to the achievements of full benchmark credentials (associate degree or certificates), but also to achievements *between* levels. Community colleges serve a diverse population that includes students who attend for different reasons—to upgrade specific skills they need for their jobs, for example—not necessarily for the purpose of reaching any benchmark credential. The model measures the value of this education, which may be lower than the achievement of a full academic degree or certificate credential, but still acknowledges the fact that it too yields monetary benefits as it raises the skill level of the worker and enhances the productivity of the workforce. This makes him/her more valuable to employers.

So, the model recognizes that there is a substantial difference between attending college for two years and earning the associate degree or a certificate, and attending for two years and *not* earning these benchmarks. Both have value, but earning the credential has more value, all else being equal. As such, we account for returns to achieving full credentials by applying what we call a "ceremonial" boost to the attainment of specific goals, such as reaching and receiving a degree or certificate. This ceremonial boost is permitted in the literature and is used to dampen the earnings curve such that returns to intermediate steps of education are on average lower than those that accrue to students who actually achieve a degree.[5]

The marketplace rewards even a few hours of successful study, and certainly recognizes the accomplishments of the student who enrolls simply to improve his or her skills or otherwise enhance their career. If a worker takes a four-week course at a local college on the most up-to-date tractor mechanics, he becomes more proficient in a certain aspect of his occupation as a result of that training, even though no qualification is awarded. The market recognizes the value of these added skills in terms of earnings differentials, which is captured and measured in the impact model. Of course, we would not expect returns as great as those that accrue to students who achieve full credentials.

Educational Pursuits

In addition to profiling the students themselves, we also account for differences in their educational pursuits in the one-year data snapshot from the colleges. The educational pursuits can vary quite widely. Some students are full-time and others attend only part-time. They all pursue different academic or vocational objectives and they are either degree-seeking or noncredit (workforce) students. For many colleges, a significant percentage of the student headcount is noncredit workforce students who attend for shorter periods of time. More than half of the students are gainfully employed while attending. The average across colleges in the 2017 database was 67 percent employed; in 2016 it was 69 percent; in 2015, 66 percent; in 2014, 66 percent; 2013, 67 percent; and in 2012 it was 70 percent employed.[6]

But it is not just being employed that counts in the calculation of the opportunity cost—what the students forgo in terms of earnings by choosing to attend school instead of working. Also factored in is the difference between what they actually earn relative to what they could earn if not attending school. While attending, these employed students lost an estimated 31 percent of their earning potential because of the types of jobs they hold compared to the nonstudent population.[7] We found this by comparing the earnings of occupations students are *likely to enter* while attending college to their full earnings potential of the *entering occupations* in their fields with only a basic level of education and little or no experience. Nonworking students obviously lose 100 percent of their earning potential and, therefore, incur a much higher opportunity cost.

Many students also transfer to a four-year university or another higher-education institution, while others remain in residence during the whole analysis year as continuing students pursuing their associate degrees, certificates, or eventual transfer to four-year universities. In the EIS, all of these differences are sorted out, and the weighted average economic gains in the region *with* the education supplied during the analysis year (*ex post*) and *without* it (*ex ante*) are measured and compared.[8]

What to Look for in an EIS

Apart from the common elements listed above, the following is essentially a "what to look for" checklist to clarify whether a study answers the questions that the college is paying for:

- An EIS should have a *regional analysis component* that measures the impact a college has on the region it serves.
- All of the regional results should be *net*, not *gross*, measures, and they should ask the question: is the region economically better off with or without the college in its midst?
- An EIS should measure the *alumni (or productivity) effect*, which captures the extent to which past students continue to contribute to the quantity and quality of the regional workforce.
- An EIS should have an *investment analysis component* that confirms whether it makes economic sense for the students to attend and/or for taxpayers to fund the colleges. The results should be expressed as discounted cash flows. Are the students and taxpayers better off with or without the college carrying out its mission?

The first three bullet points in the checklist above will be discussed and explained below in this chapter. The last bullet point will be discussed in chapter 3.

THE REGIONAL ANALYSIS

Now we turn to the first item in the checklist, which is the regional component. This component essentially measures the change in economic activity of the region as a result of college's operation and student spending during the analysis year, plus the sum total of the regional economic activity generated from the embedded credit hours earned by the past students that add value each year. It is also a measurement that the college should always seek to increase. The discussion below is slightly but hopefully not too technical, so please bear with us as we sort it all out.

An EIS should have a *regional analysis component* that measures the impact a college has on the region it serves.

Input-Output Analysis and the Multiplier Effect

The regional component of the data tells us the current measure of the GRP at the beginning of the analysis year. This is our *benchmark*. The model then measures the extent to which the GRP increases at the end of the analysis year as a result of the activities of the college in spending its budget. For the not-so-economically-inclined, this analytical process consists of applying a fairly sophisticated input/output (I/O) analysis that provides a comprehensive picture of all the transactions in a regional economy.

The input is the budget for the analysis year, the output is how the college spends it—inside the region or outside the region—and what that spending does for the regional economy.

The college does what it is designed to do: it dispenses education. In turn, dispensing that education is done through several lines of study—i.e., the programs offered. This college budget is spent on the salaries for faculty and staff serving those programs, on infrastructure, buildings and equipment, and for miscellaneous supplies purchased from the vendors, regional or national. All that spending generates a multiplier effect, which is what the I/O analysis measures. Without going too deeply into the weeds, the multiplier analysis sorts all of this out as described further below.

The regional analysis begins with the selection of a geographical region of influence. The colleges tell us the counties those regions include. This, however, can be a political process with consequences. In some states it is easy—the regions "belonging" to individual colleges are set by law, as in Wisconsin. There, the 15 community colleges divide the counties in the state so that no college's region overlaps with another. A region can be as small as one or two counties (e.g., North Carolina with 100 counties and 58 colleges). In other states, one college may serve several counties (e.g., Texas has 254 counties and only 50 community colleges). It varies.

Politically, and *if* a choice of region is possible, a college would want the region to be larger if a bond election is at stake. There would be more taxpayers to contribute to the cause. The tradeoff, of course, is that there would be more taxpayers to potentially vote no, and the college may be seen as a smaller fish in a bigger pond.

Technically, a region should be functional and encompass dominance as its own labor market—it should not be defined by administrative boundaries.

Practically, most economic impact analyses use administrative (county) boundaries to define regions of influence, because that is how the relevant data are being reported. The discrepancy between the results found with administrative regions versus functional economic regions, however, are small enough to be considered insignificant. So, the Emsi model too defines regions along administrative boundaries.

The purpose of the I/O analysis is to derive the multiplier effect, best described as a ripple effect in the economy. Envision a pebble thrown into still water and notice where the ripples in the water radiate out from the point of impact. The ripples are bigger close to the point of impact and weaken as they radiate out. The pebble, for purposes of this discussion, is the college budget. As the budget is being spent, the point of impact is the first round of spending, or the initial spending of the college budget during the analysis year. The ripples occur as the recipients of the first round of spending, in turn, spend *their* newfound income, and so on in successively smaller iterations.

The *initial* impact of the college budget is the amount the college spends on payroll.

The *direct* impact is the amount the college spends on vendors in the region, as in the college purchases office supplies from a local office supply store, which then needs to restock its shelves.

The *indirect* portion is characterized by iterations (ripples) of subsequent spending by the recipients of the college's initial spending. And again, so it goes in successively smaller iterations.

The *induced* effect is a component part of the multiplier calculated by the I/O, and is measured separately by the extent to which the spending by the college triggers an overall improvement in the workforce productivity.

In the end, the I/O analysis and the multiplier effect it generates demonstrate the economic significance of a college on a defined region. The region has a gross GRP of $X billion. Of that total, the presence of the college in that region explains, or accounts for Y percent of that GRP. In other words, were it not for the existence of the college in that region, therefore, the GRP would have been Y percent smaller.

Net vs. Gross

Next in the what-to-look-for-in-an-EIS endeavor is the all-important observation that the results should be *net*, not *gross*, measures.

A convincing research effort on this very topic was done in 2006 by authors from Vanderbilt University, the University of Chicago, and Yale University.[9] Here is their abstract, which signals the issues we consider so important in conducting an EIS for colleges:

> This essay describes methodological approaches and pitfalls common to studies of the economic impact of colleges and universities. Such studies often claim local benefits that imply annualized rates of return on local investment exceeding 100 percent. We address problems in these studies pertaining to the specification of the counterfactual, the definition of the local area, the identification of "new" expenditures, the tendency to double-count economic impacts, the role of local taxes, and the omission of local spillover benefits from enhanced human capital created by higher education, and offer several suggestions for improvement. If these economic impact studies were conducted at the level of accuracy most institutions require of

faculty research, their claims of local economic benefits would not be so preposterous, and, as a result, trust in and respect for higher-education officials would be enhanced.[10]

This topic was briefly introduced in the previous chapter. Presidents and governing boards need to know the differences between gross and net measures. It is paramount that everyone fully understands that only the *net* measures count as impacts. "Net" reflects the level of economic activity in the region that a president can confidently claim as uniquely attributable to the college. All other measures larger than that are not impacts; they merely rearrange the furniture, or count "impacts" from monies spent that could just as easily be spent on other things.

As documented in Watson et al., economic "impact" studies fall into three categories:[11] contributions, GRP, or true economic impacts. In a nutshell, the problem is that almost all of the studies reviewed *claim to estimate economic impacts* regardless of the distinct nuances. Too often, presidents and governing boards have been led to believe that the studies they received and paid for measured impacts when, in fact, they did not.

The three types of economic activity studies are nested within one another. Contributions are the largest, with GRP being the next largest, and impacts being the smallest as shown in figure 2.1.

The most common type of economic activity study undertaken is a *contributions* analysis. The error committed in many if not most of the studies we looked at before building the Emsi model is that they were, in fact, contributions studies that were almost universally *mislabeled as impact studies*. We suspect that the consultants *intended* to measure impacts, but they just did not explicitly account for the gross versus net differences.

In all fairness, we also made this error when we embarked on the project to build our state-of-the-art model, but caught it in time before any studies were released. There were mistakes that did require changes in methodology, but this, thankfully, was not one of them.

The obvious question is this: "when advocating for a college, wouldn't a college president just want the biggest results?" The answer is an emphatic no. If all a president and governing board want is the largest possible numbers, then they should contract specifically for an advocacy study that shows the college's *gross contributions* to the re-

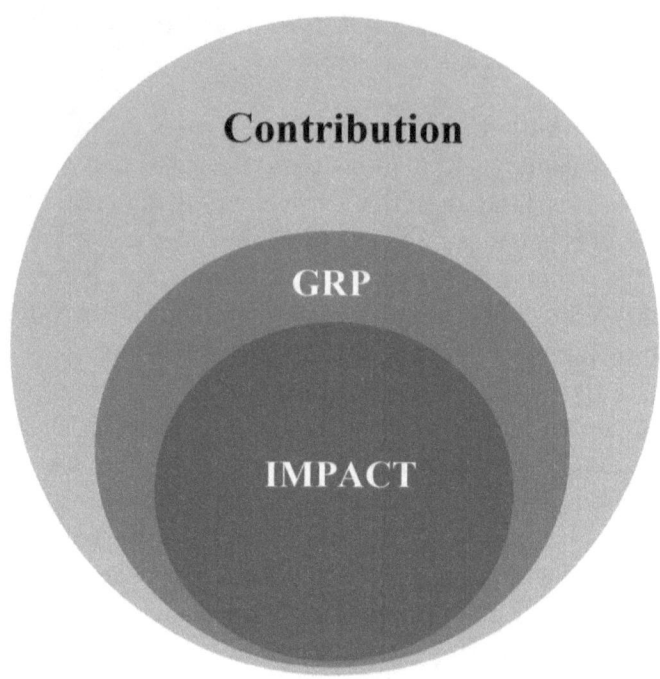

Figure 2.1. Gross vs. net impacts. Kjell A. Christophersen, Tim Nadreau, and Aaron Olanie, "The Rights and Wrongs of Economic Impact Analysis for Colleges and Universities," Emsi blog, January 7, 2014.

gion, regardless of where the money came from. If they do so, however, they should know that such a contributions study would surely be discredited *especially if it is misrepresented as an impact study*. And that misrepresentation is quite common because the analysts do not know they are, in fact, misrepresenting the contributions as impacts. When this happens, the stakeholders are misled, and the college unwittingly risks having the exact opposite of the intent of the study happen— exposure and negative press. That, of course, is a political side effect to avoid.

If, on the other hand, the college leaders want a solid and defensible true EIS, they need to know the differences between contributions, GRP, and net impacts. In the end, commissioning a net impact study enhances rather than detracts from the community goodwill because the numbers, although smaller, will have a much higher value and be much easier to defend.

In a contributions study, every dollar spent by the college is measured along with the associated multiplier effect, regardless of where that money comes from. Think of it as a zero-sum game. The money that makes up the college budget comes from a variety of sources, some from inside the region, some from outside. The students pay tuition and fees, the state funds the college through state appropriations or property taxes (or both), some money comes from Federal sources (grants, Pell, Perkins, etc.), and some comes from private donors, foundations, and the like. When tallied up, all that money comprises the college budget, which is spent during the analysis year.

A college that spends a budget of $100 million with a calculated multiplier of 2 *contributes* $200 million to the regional economy. This is a *contribution* measure; not an *impact* measure. In fact, if we did a similar contributions analysis for every institution with a payroll in that region (be it a sawmill, a hospital, or a manufacturing plant), the sum of these contributions would far exceed the true volume of dollars circulating in the regional economy. Contribution studies, therefore, do not consider the "broken window" principle (discussed in the previous chapter), i.e., the sacrificed alternative spending or the crowding-out effects of allocating a budget between alternative and competing ends.

If a college requests an impact study but instead receives a contributions study *labeled* as an impact study, the burden is on the president and the governing board to recognize this as such and send it back for some serious revisions. A contribution study vastly overstates the true impacts of a college.

Less frequent in occurrence is the GRP analysis. This approach goes *part* of the way toward a net measure as it examines the fraction of total value added in a region that stems from a particular industry or firm, but not all the way. One can think of value added as the increased value an industry or firm produces as it restructures and mixes the inputs used in its production process. In a bakery, flour, milk, and yeast have less value on their own than when they are mixed together and baked into bread. The additional value that the bread has over and above its intermediate and separable inputs is the value added by the bakery.

For a college, the inputs are the students, the programs taught, and the resulting increased productivity in the workforce manifested in higher earnings.

Conducting a GRP analysis of every firm in the region would sum to the total GRP of the region. It is, therefore, a smaller subset of the broader contribution analysis. Notice, however, that this analysis still does not answer the question of how much of that value added is solely attributable to the bakery, or how much money would be lost to the economy if the bakery had never existed. This analysis still suffers from the failure to account for the opportunity cost and crowding-out effects, though perhaps not to the same extent that the contribution analysis does.

Where does the money come from? What constitutes new money to the region? That is considered next—*impacts*—the narrowest of all economic activity analyses. This measure is a subset of GRP. We have now arrived at what the college actually needs from the EIS, how much it *uniquely* accounts for all economic activities in the region.

Here is a look at what this means practically.

Only the money brought into the region from *outside* should be fully counted. This means most federal dollars, money from foundations located outside the region, money from state tax appropriations paid by taxpayers living outside the region, money from students paying tuition who live outside the region, etc. would be included in the count. This is *new* money flowing to the region, *only because the college is located there*. If the college did not exist, this money would not be coming into the region from these sources.

The portion of the money generated for the college budget from *inside* the region is backed out because it is *not* new money flowing into the region. This includes the property-tax portion plus the money coming from inside-the-region taxpayers being allocated for the state-tax appropriations to support the college.

Most of the local dollars received, and then spent by the college, are simply a reshuffling of local resources, and reshuffling does not constitute an impact. If a study includes local money in the college budget, the reader should be wary.[12] Watson et al. define impacts as

> the value added portion of revenues that are generated by an industry from sales outside the region (exports), the value added portion of sales to visitors that come to the region (tourist spending), and the value added from locals who would have spent their money on goods from outside the region had the industry [firm] not been present inside the region (import substitution).[13]

To put it all together, let's assume for a moment that the college has the (hypothetical) budget of $100 million to spend on college operations during the analysis year (faculty and staff payroll, vendors inside and outside the regional economy). Moving from gross to net, we begin with only counting the money spent inside the economy. Money spent outside leaks out and is not counted in the regional impact.

Suppose that furthermore, the data show that the college spends 80 percent of the $100 million budget *inside* the region during the analysis year. Most of that amount is spent on the payroll, but a significant portion is also spent on local vendors. The spending on nonlocal vendors is not counted as a regional impact.

The regional impact, in this case, amounts to $80 million.[14] The indirect spending occurs as the recipients of the $80 million (faculty and staff plus local vendors) spend *that* money on *their* payroll and vendors. This cycle continues in successively smaller iterations as discussed above, all contributing to a multiple of the original $80 million spent by the college inside the region.

If the multiplier is measured at, say 2, the total indirect plus induced spending impact amounts to another $80 million spent in the regional economy, or simply the direct impact of $80 million x 2 = $160 million.[15] At a first glance, therefore, the presence of the college adds $160 million to the GRP.

The I/O analysis just described is technically correct—it is precisely the approach taken by many past studies, at least those recognizing that the budget is spent on *both* local and nonlocal vendors. The $160 million is what these analysts claim the impact of the college is on the region it serves. This still reflects, however, a mechanical use of the I/O methodology—not incorrectly, but mechanical nonetheless—whereby the results are presented as true impact measures by many analysts. In fact, the $160 million still measures contributions, not impacts. Presidents and governing boards should be well aware of these pitfalls.

Next, in table 2.1 we will consider the *sources* of revenues. To summarize, we started with the $100 million budget, and then we backed out the 20 percent spent outside the region as the first step in our journey from gross to net, leaving us with $80 million as the first starting point for estimating the impacts above. The *sources* of the $80 million revenue now become very important. Recall, we should only count *new* money flowing into the region—money that would not have flowed to the region were it not for the presence of the college.

So, what constitutes new money? Well, most of the federal money is new to the region. Students from outside the region paying tuition and fees and living expenses is new money. These will all have an impact on the region when spent there and should be counted as part of the $100 million. But to include dollars that would have been spent in the region anyway would simply be tantamount to only rearranging the furniture. State funding—the biggest funding contributors to community colleges—falls into this category. We must identify and separate out this money.

How we do this is simple. In most states, the taxpayers support colleges in two ways: property taxes collected from inside-the-region taxpayers, and state appropriations. The main adjustment, therefore, is to back out the portion of the property taxes that are paid by inside-the-region taxpayers and allocated to the college, plus a small portion of the state appropriation funding.[16] By backing these two out the economic spending impacts and the multiple thereof generated by the college are much smaller as they are measured from a significantly smaller pool of money in the budget.

Suppose 40 percent of the original $100 million budget comes from the state taxpayers ($40 million) of which half is in the form of appropriations, and the other half ($20 million) comes from inside-the-region property taxes. We back the latter portion out—the $20 million property taxes—entirely. In addition, we back out a portion of the state appropriations equal to the ratio of state taxpayers inside the region relative to all the state taxpayers. Say that amounts to 5 percent of the $40 million from the taxpayers; so, we back out an additional $2 million. Of

Table 2.1. Starting Point for Impact Calculation

Original budget (millions)	$100
Spent outside region, 20%	$20
Spent inside region	$80
Back out property taxes	$20
Back out state tax appropriations	$2
Starting point	$58

the initial $100 million budget, therefore, the calculation shown in table 2.1 generates the starting point for calculating the net impacts.

As shown, the reduced spending budget *starting point* for the amount subjected to the multiplier calculation is only $58 million representing new money to the region because the college is located there, not the full $80 million. The *net impact* when the budget is spent, therefore, is $58 million x 2 (multiplier) = $116 million, a far cry from the gross "impact" of $160 million as measured above. We call this net impact the "institutional operations effect"—or the net added income generated in the region because of the college's payroll and its local purchases for supplies and services.

For many economic impact studies, the operations effect marks the end of the study. But it is not; there is a lot more we can add to the economic impacts of a college. The spending impact measure is not only confined to the college budget. Students and visitors spend too.[17] Colleges attract students who spend a lot of money on books, lodging, entertainment, and eating and drinking in the region while attending the college. When tallied up with the multiplier effect factored in, student and visitor spending can be shown to have a profound and measurable impact on the regional economy.

To be fair, many other studies also add in student spending and some added visitor spending. But, they almost uniformly do so by counting *all* the students who attend, not just those who enroll from outside the region. True, all students spend, but only a relatively small fraction of them should be counted as bringing new money to the region. In fact, nationwide, less than 18 percent of a typical student body at a community college comes from outside the region over the last seven years.[18] This group is comprised of international students and students from adjacent counties or from elsewhere in the United States.

For a typical community college in the United States, therefore, about 82 percent of the student body is from the local community-college region, and their spending should *not* be counted as an impact on the local region. Their spending would occur in the region regardless of whether they attend the college. In fact, it could be argued that they would have spent even more in the local region had they not attended the college. This is because they would probably be gainfully employed and would, therefore, spend even more. A properly conducted EIS should count only the 18 percent of student spending as contributing to the economic impact.

Next (and moving beyond the spending impacts), there are three additional counterfactuals to account for in a true economic impact study: the ability bias, alternative education effect, and the substitution effect, also known as the importation of labor, which is sometimes easier to understand. These, summarized in table 2.2 and briefly described in the sections below, all reduce the other (and main) component of the economic impacts—*higher earnings*—experienced in the regional workforce because of the education the students receive.

To set the stage, and to simplify things, suppose we have a college located inside a defined geographical region serving a total headcount of 15,000 students during the analysis year, students who remain in the region and become gainfully employed there after their studies. These students each achieve, on average, 11 CHEs, for a total of 165,000 CHEs. In addition, there is an average increase in earnings of some $275 per CHE, which translates to a little more than $45 million for the analysis year for the student body. The following sections describe each counterfactual separately. The question is whether this full measure of gross earnings should be included as the starting point for the multiplier calculation.

We begin with the ability bias. Higher earnings by the exiting students are closely correlated to education levels. As statistics show, earnings increase as education levels rise—and that increase is embedded in the average value of $275 per CHE in the table above. If, however, we

Table 2.2. How to Calculate Counterfactuals

Students, headcount	15,000
CHEs achieved per student	11
Total CHEs achieved during analysis year	165,000
Average increase in earnings per CHE	$275
Gross earnings (contributions)	$45.375.000
Ability bias, 10%	$248
Increased earnings, less ability bias	$40,837,500
Alternative education, 15%	$6,125,625
Labor substitution, 50%	$20,418,750
Net impact, adjusting for all counterfactuals	$14,293,125

interpret the correlation between education and earnings to mean that *all* of the returns should be attributed to schooling, that measure would certainly be upwardly biased. It is important to isolate how much of the return can be attributed to *causation*—the underlying, but contributing reasons for the higher earnings, or what we call the "ability bias." As the saying goes, "correlation does not equal causation." The return attributed to schooling must be discounted to reflect this bias.

The question is, by how much should we discount the higher earnings? That all of the earnings increase cannot be attributed to the education only should be obvious. It is certainly obvious to the naysayers critical of overinflated metrics who will rightfully call to task any study failing to account for this counterfactual. The ability bias should be estimated and netted out because some students do not necessarily depend on the presence of the college for their increased earnings. Other factors, such as natural ability and family background, should be front and center in the analyst's EIS protocol.

Students endowed with a high natural ability tend to get a higher level of education than less-gifted students. They achieve their education levels more easily because the college is present in the region. If the college was *not* present, however, these students would still be getting their education elsewhere anyway. The education level achieved by the student body at large is upwardly biased by the more naturally gifted students who do not depend on the presence of the college in that region. And this is what we correct for.

Likewise, students who have engaged parents and/or family connections have an easier time, not only with school and program choices, but also in landing the good jobs that command the highest wages, regardless of the presence of the college in that region. This too generates an upward bias in the education levels achieved.

In 2001, we commissioned a literature review study to determine the magnitude of the ability bias assumption for the Emsi EIS.[19] This study became the source for the assumption that 10 percent of the higher earnings attributable to the education received should be backed out because they were not attributable solely to the college. Based on this research, we therefore discounted the $275 annual increase in earnings per credit hour equivalent achieved for one year's worth of schooling by a 10 percent ability bias to reflect only a net of $248 of the higher earnings per CHE that the college can claim as attributable to the education offered. For the entire region the gross increased earnings total, therefore, is nearly $41 million net of the ability bias, or 165,000 CHEs x $248 = $40.8 million.

Net of the ability bias, the starting point is now lowered to $40.8 million. Next is the "alternative education" counterfactual. What is this, exactly? It is simply the answer to the question of *"how many students would be able to avail themselves of a similar alternative education and find gainful employment in the region if the college did not exist or if it shut down?"* Counting the impacts from these students would be in error because the absence of the college does not mean that they would be deprived of their education—they would simply attend elsewhere. They can afford to.[20] The college cannot take credit for the benefits that these students generate for the region once they enter the workforce because they would generate similar benefits even if the college did not exist. The rest of the student body, on the other hand, *would be* deprived because it would be too expensive to enroll elsewhere, or the next available college may be simply too far away.

An economic impact study would be in error if this counterfactual were not included in the model. This was clearly pointed out in the 2006 working paper by economists at Vanderbilt University.[21] We included this variable in our state-of-the-art model even before the Vanderbilt study was published. The problem, however, was that we had difficulties, just like the Vanderbilt researchers, in structuring an assumption based on published data because others had not included this phenomenon in their impact analyses for colleges and universities.

> Establishing a counterfactual for a college is challenging. First, institutions of higher education do not appear and disappear quickly. Conceptualizing Boston without Harvard (founded 1636) is difficult. The annual number of colleges opening or closing is modest. Because most colleges start small and grow slowly over time, it is also usually impossible to identify a short period of time over which the difference between the absence and presence of a college on its local area might be discerned.[22]

In the beginning we searched high and low for some appropriate data to structure an assumption to reflect this phenomenon and then, when we found some, we built submodels and ran regression analyses. But in the end, the fit just was not there, so we simply hardwired 15 percent to reflect the number of students to back out from the impact calculations. This was done because the need to recognize this important variable in the analysis outweighed the avoidance of doing so *because* of the lack of data. As a result, we backed out yet another $6.1 million as indicated in table 2.2.[23]

Finally, we still had one more major adjustment to make before arriving at a true net measure—the labor substitution counterfactual.

To reiterate, an impact analysis is all about measuring the sum total of economic activity in a region with and without the college in its midst.[24] As a college releases newly minted graduates and non-degree-seeking students back into the regional workforce, the region as a whole becomes more productive because of the skills the students acquired while at the college. That increased productivity is the reason why employers are willing to pay higher wages, which translates into the GRP. The more the GRP grows as a result of the college's activities, the more the college can take the credit.

A college cannot claim credit for all the productivity gain in the regional economy, even after adjusting for the two counterfactuals discussed above. Employers do not hire workers from the college *only*. In fact, many of their employees are hired from outside the region—they are imported. Therefore, if a college fails to supply *all* of the skills demanded, the regional employers would not simply roll over and make do without them. They will instead recruit workers from outside the region—substituting out-of-region workers for in-region workers. For this reason, a college cannot claim that all that productivity would be lost to the region if the college did not exist.

The burning question, of course, is how much of the increased productivity *can* be claimed by a college? And here again, the challenge was to find the data needed to structure an assumption. Similar to the alternative education counterfactual, therefore, we very much needed to *recognize* this as an important phenomenon in the model. And so, we added a default assumption of 50 percent, meaning that regional employers would hire out-of-region workers to the tune of 50 percent if the college did not supply the skilled workforce needed. In this case, the remaining 50 percent is the impact we measure as attributable to the college. In table 2.2, therefore, we only claim 50 percent of the $40.8 million worth of higher earnings as attributable to the college, or

$20.4 million. The other half is attributable to workers hired from outside the region.

Given the choice, some colleges used the default assumptions of 50 percent, but others did not. They were given the opportunity to override the default assumption, and many colleges do because they too want to generate accurate and defensible impact measures. They know the hiring patterns of regional employers. Urban colleges, for example, often change the assumption from the default of 50/50 to as much as 10/90 to reflect that urban area employers have many more options when shopping around for their skill needs and they hire fewer workers from the local college. In this case, the college takes credit for only 10 percent of the local productivity gain. Some rural colleges, on the other hand, change the assumption the other way, sometimes as high as 75/25 because there the regional employers have fewer options and, therefore, hire a higher percentage of workers from the local college.[25]

In the end, having gone through meticulous counterfactual calculations to ensure that we show net impacts for the analysis year and do not simply rearrange the furniture, the college can confidently claim that nearly $14.3 million worth of initial annual higher earnings is attributable to the presence of the college in the region. This net impact is far lower than the original $45.3 million gross "impact" shown in table 2.2. This (net number) is defensible before a critical audience. But the college president must know the ins and outs of how it was derived, and also that other studies used for comparison purposes may not have gone through this process.

Sales vs. Income

Not a counterfactual, but it is worth mentioning that the regional impact results should be expressed in terms of income, not sales. Many studies express the regional results in sales terms (typically the ones we describe as contributions studies), which generate much higher and, presumably more impressive, results when analyzing college impacts. This would simply be a deceptive metric, particularly if analyzing a college in a defined small region. Consider the following example taken from the Emsi EIS:[26]

Two individuals spend $50,000 each in the economic region. One visits a local auto dealer and purchases a new luxury automobile. The other undergoes a medical procedure at the local hospital. In terms of direct economic impact, both have spent $50,000, and the auto dealer and hospital have made sales worth $50,000 each. So far so good. However, the sales have very different meanings to the local economy.

Of the $50,000 spent for the luxury automobile, perhaps as little as $10,000 remains in the county as salesperson commissions and auto dealer income (part of the economic region's overall income), while the remaining $40,000 leaves the area for Detroit or Tokyo as wholesale payment for the new automobile.

Contrast this to the hospital expenditure. Here perhaps $40,000 appears as physician, nurse, and assorted hospital employee wages (part of the region's overall earnings), while only $10,000 leaves the area to pay for hospital supplies, or to help amortize building and equipment loans. In terms of sales, both have the same impact, while in terms of income, the former has one-fourth the impact of the latter.

The regional sales numbers are more impressive because they are higher, especially when applied to an industry where most of the money leaks out. If 80 percent of the sales numbers leak out of the economy, they cannot be counted as impacts attributable to the company. They would not reflect impacts at all since those dollars are not even in the regional economy.

The fundamental reason we use income rather than sales is this: sales may be bringing money into the economy, but until that money starts rippling through the regional economy, it has no impact. The allocation of the sales dollars to employees in the form of income is the beginning of the ripple effects. A reader of an EIS should be on guard if sales numbers are being reported. Note, however, that if the region is very large, such as a state or several states, then the results will be less overstated because less money leaks out of a large economy as opposed to a small economy.

ALUMNI EFFECT

And now we are done with the "bad" news reflected by all of the counterfactuals we invoke to generate a true net estimate of a college's economic impact on the region. It is time for some good news. We still have to derive the number the president and governing board can confidently publish and "brag" about until it is time for the next EIS study. An EIS should measure the *alumni effect*, which captures the extent to which past students continue to contribute to the quantity and quality of the regional workforce.

Enter the productivity effect, or the alumni effect discussed earlier. This effect is simply the value of the cumulative number of CHEs *embedded in the regional workforce* over the past 30 years. These CHEs add value each year for which the college can claim credit, because they do not dissipate once the students are released into the workforce. In addition, nonlabor effects such as transfer payments and higher business profits, etc., also come with the territory as the students earn more and are more productive in the workforce. Multiply all of this by the cumulative number of CHEs embedded in the regional workforce, add the multiplier effect, and all told, we derive an estimate of the annual impact of this year's current student body *plus* the impact of the alumni now gainfully employed in the regional workforce. This (larger) number is also a metric that tells the stakeholders how much smaller the economy would be if the college did not exist.[27]

The alumni effect is the single-most significant Emsi addition to the EIS model. It adds far more to the overall impact of colleges than the amount we "lose" because we express the impacts in net, not gross terms. Most community colleges have served their local regions for 40 years or even longer (since the early 60s), and that presence has measurably impacted both the quantity and quality of the regional workforce over time. Students who attended the colleges 30 years ago who may still be actively engaged in the regional workforce are adding value every year because of their education.[28]

Think for a moment about this—the value of education does not dissipate the moment it has been completed. A sawmill produces dimension lumber, and the value of the product dissipates the moment it is sold. A hospital heals people, and the value dissipates when the healing is complete. Education, on the other hand, is different. Its value remains with the student for as long as he or she is in the workforce, adding incrementally to the economic activities in a region each year. The model is accounting for this dynamic by estimating the cumulative number of CHEs still embedded and active in the regional workforce during one single year of analysis using statistics on out-migration, student achievements, retirement and death, and unemployment.

Since each CHE has a measurable value, it provides the estimate of how much the education for which the college can claim credit is worth. We aptly call this the "productivity effect," and it is akin to the Energizer bunny—it keeps on going. When the students exit the colleges with more skills than they had before, this is valued in the marketplace with higher earnings, not just for the first year they are employed, but for as long as they remain in the regional workforce. As workers transition from one job to the next in their careers, that incremental value attributable to their community college education remains with them until they retire.

CONCLUSION

This chapter has focused primarily on one of the two components of the economic impact study—the regional component. The second component—investment analysis from the perspectives of the students and taxpayers—is covered in the next chapter. The regional component is the more dominant of the two because it measures what *all* analysts include—the impacts in terms of dollars and cents that the college has on the region it serves. The investment analysis only begins to confirm that the monies spent by the college are not wasted. And they are not wasted so long as the investments analysis results from the taxpayer and student perspectives meet or exceed threshold levels.[29]

Dollars-and-cents impacts, however, can have several meanings. They are not a generic measurement that describes a cause-and-effect relationship between money spent and the consequent multiplier results of that spending. The word "impact" can mean different things, but only one is right. The meaning that represents the college's regional impact is captured in the word *net*, as opposed to *gross*. Only a *net* measure should be conveyed to the stakeholders; gross impacts merely rearrange the furniture.

What we want to measure for the stakeholders is what the regional economy's GRP would look like without the college located there. Or, to put it differently, were it not for the presence of the college in that region, the regional economy would be X percent smaller. To do this properly, we must net out all of the spending that would have occurred in the region anyway, with or without the college, to derive a true measure of the spending in the region that occurred *because* the college is there doing what it does.

EISs for higher-education institutions are commissioned by both community colleges and universities. The models, however, are different in their application, because the institutions are different, as are the interpretation of the results. Those differences need to be understood in their proper context. And that context is more complex for community colleges than it is for universities. Community colleges serve a wider swath of students than the universities, including much higher numbers of students who enroll and take classes, but do not seek any credential. These are the noncredit students who attend for only short periods of time to refresh and/or update their skills. For a typical community college, the noncredit students comprise a significant percentage of the student body headcount.

Good is the fact that community colleges are sufficiently supple to accommodate noncredit students. This needs to be better communicated.

Bad is the fact that these students, forming part of the total student body headcount, dilute the statistics on graduation rates. This too needs to be better communicated.

NOTES

1. The GRP is the market value of all final goods and services produced in the geographical region specified during the analysis year.
2. Michael Mitchell, M. Leachman, K. Masterson, and S. Waxman, "Unkept Promises: State Cuts to Higher Education Threaten Access and Equity," Center on Budget and Policy Priorities, October 4, 2018, https://www.cbpp.org/research/state-budget-and-tax/unkept-promises-state-cuts-to-higher-education-threaten-access-and. To be correct here, while college presidents' proposed budgets may not be fully funded, it is the difference between the actual budgets received and fully funded according to the colleges' requests that

becomes reported as budget cuts. According to the census of government data and the Integrated Postsecondary Education Data System (IPEDS) historic data, these are technically not budget cuts, of course, just less than what was requested.

3. The average age for community college students in the United States is about 27 years of age (Emsi EIS database). This is a composite average of credit and nondegree seeking.

4. If retirement occurs at 65 years of age, then 65 minus the average age gives us the remaining time horizon for the rest of the earnings function for the cohort being analyzed.

5. Economic theory holds that workers who acquire education credentials send a signal to employers about their ability level. This phenomenon is commonly known as the "sheepskin" or "signaling" effect. The ceremonial boosts applied to the achievement of degrees in the Emsi college impact model are derived from David Jaeger and Marianne Page, "Degrees Matter: New Evidence on Sheepskin Effects in the Returns to Education," *Review of Economics and Statistics* 78, no. 4 (November 1996): 733–40.

6. Emsi EIS database

7. This is a national statistic. Emsi's goal is to make this state- and even region-specific in 2019.

8. Emsi's data is curated from sources such as QCEW (Quarterly Census of Employment and Wages) and OES (Occupational and Employment Statistics) and is updated quarterly. All totaled, we invoke some 100 federal and state data sources in our proprietary data. The data collected from the college is the latest audited data set available.

9. John J. Siegfried, Allen R. Sanderson, and Peter McHenry, "The Economic Impact of Colleges and Universities," Working Paper No. 6-W12, Department of Economics, Vanderbilt University, 2006.

10. Ibid.

11. Philip Watson, Joshua Wilson, Dawn Thilmany, and Susan Winter, "Determining Economic Contributions and Impacts: What Is the Difference and Why Do We Care?" *Journal of Regional Analysis and Policy* 37, no. 2 (2007): 1–15.

12. Technically, the Emsi model counts a portion of the regional money received because the impact from consumers spending that money and the impact from the college spending that money may be different. We account for that difference.

13. Ibid.

14. To keep it simple, this example is a mix of initial (payroll for employees working in the region) and direct (spending on vendors inside the region).

15. Most studies claim all the institution's expenditures and then use some predefined multiplier to calculate the total impact.

16. The portion of the state appropriations backed out is the portion allocated to support the college from state taxes paid by inside-the-region residents.

17. Maybe 1 in 100 colleges will have a visitor spending impact. Usually community colleges don't attract enough visitors to make it worthwhile to measure the impacts. If they do have many visitors from outside the region, they typically do not have the data for the analysts to perform a credible analysis.

18. Emsi EIS database

19. Chris Molitor and Duane Leigh, *Estimating the Returns to Schooling: Calculating the Difference Between Causation and Correlation*. Report prepared for CCbenefits, Inc., March 2001.

20. Online education is increasing as well.

21. Siegfried, Sanderson, and McHenry, "The Economic Impact of Colleges and Universities."

22. Ibid.

23. The alternative education counterfactual is fairly unique to the Emsi model; it is rarely addressed in our competitors' studies. Hardwiring this assumption made it necessary to run an analysis in the model to determine how sensitive the overall results were to an incremental change in the assumption up or down from the base case assumption of 15 percent.

24. There are those who claim that a taxpayer-funded college reduces the GRP because, after all, colleges occupy a lot of property that otherwise would have been on the property tax rolls.

25. Most impact studies sidestep the issue by ignoring the effect altogether. A study that fails to account for this effect as a counterfactual, however, would be in error . . . so says the literature.

26. It is only when a national study involving all 1,200 community colleges is conducted that sales and earnings would be equal.

27. The increased productivity is a result of the education offered at the college. But it is also generated in other ways. A farm manager, for example, may increase the productivity of his farm because he now knows how to utilize drones and financial software.

28. On the horizon for the EIS is to figure out which industries the alumni work in and then measure what part of those industries' value added is a result of the education provided by the college. That way industries would know how much they are being benefited by the colleges they recruit from.

29. The investment analysis from the perspectives of students and taxpayers is not an efficiency analysis, as will be discussed in later chapters. In fact, it may be the case that if the taxpayers invested more, the ROI would go down (or it

could go up). We are simply measuring that for this cohort of students—this is the return on investment for students and taxpayers.

3

THE INVESTMENT COMPONENT OF AN ECONOMIC IMPACT STUDY

Who Invests?

In this chapter, we switch to the investment component of the economic impact study (EIS) in our "what to look for" checklist. An EIS should have an *investment analysis component* that confirms whether it makes economic sense for the students to attend and/or for taxpayers to fund the colleges. The results should be expressed as discounted cash flows. Are the students and taxpayers better off with or without the college carrying out its mission?

The regional impact discussion in the previous chapter is all about spending by the college and the students and the higher earnings the students enjoy when they enter the workforce. Now we add what it means to students and taxpayers when they make their investments in education. That meaning becomes personal, at least for the students. They are the ones who incur the out-of-pocket cash outlays for tuition and fees, future payments on student loans, and the opportunity costs of not working because they are in school instead. For the taxpayers it becomes less personal because it is embroiled in politics, where the majority rules and the minority has no choice but to comply.

Investments are not about spending; rather, they are about measuring the returns—the net benefits—received because of the students' choice to invest in their education, or the taxpayers' choice to fund the colleges. To summarize it into CliffsNotes, the students benefit from the higher earnings received as a result of the education received. The higher earnings are *the* incentive for the students to invest in their own education. Taxpayers who fund the colleges also enjoy benefits in the form of added tax revenues (or higher tax collections) from the higher earnings. These added tax revenues (albeit far more hidden) are *the* incentive that paves the way for the state tax appropriations that fund the colleges.

THRESHOLD VALUES AND THE DISCOUNT RATE

There are thresholds that define the attractiveness of these investments. The student and taxpayer investments are measured by way of standard benefit/cost investment analysis where the results are expressed as net present values (NPV), internal rates of return (IRR), and benefit/cost ratios (B/C). These measurements compare the present value benefits to present value costs received/incurred incrementally over time, and then collapses them into one number that tells whether the investment is worthwhile.

Any investment is economically worthwhile if the NPV is equal to $0 or higher; if the B/C ratio is equal to 1 or higher; and if the IRR is equal to the discount rate or higher.[1]

The questions answered in the investment analysis are these: (1) does it make economic sense for the students to attend college, and (2) does it make economic sense for the taxpayers to continue to fund the colleges? "Economic sense" is achieved (as above) if the present value of the future incremental benefits exceeds the present value of the costs. Practically, this means that the recipients (students and taxpayers) are better off with the investments than without them. Technically, it means that the NPV is greater than 0, the B/C ratio is greater than 1, and the IRR is greater than the opportunity cost of capital reflected by the discount rate.

The threshold values are defined as the tipping points for the students choosing to enroll or not, or, for the state taxpayers to *know* whether they are losing or gaining money from funding the colleges at a certain level. But what do the B/C ratio, NPV, and IRR measurements actually mean? Well, first of all, they all use the simple benefit and cost cash flows over time in their calculations, which yields similar results but which are expressed differently. A B/C ratio is expressed as a numerical ratio, an NPV is expressed in dollar terms, and the IRR is expressed in percentage terms. All of these measures depend on a *given discount rate*.

To fully understand the threshold values, we must also know what "a given discount rate" means. It is not the same as an interest rate. An interest rate is market-determined; a discount rate, on the other hand, is selected by the analyst using data and other investment options. The selection process can be, and often is, politically charged because every project has proponents and opponents, especially when taxpayer investments are considered. To make a project look attractive, *proponents* prefer a low discount rate because the present values of the benefits will be higher. *Opponents*, on the other hand, will argue for higher discount rates because the present value benefits will be lower and less attractive.

The point here is to inform college presidents about the importance of the discount rates chosen for the students and taxpayers. If the discount rate is on the high side and the investment analysis result still exceeds threshold values, then there is assurance that the investment is solid. That assurance has value to college presidents, however, only if they are fully aware of the rate chosen and what that means. Or, if they know it is low, the investment analysis results will be correspondingly "more attractive" and they will have the wherewithal to ask the question of how high the discount rate can go before the results switch from attractive to unattractive. This is to ward off any negative political fallout over the discount rate chosen.

So, what are the elements of a discount rate? It embeds two fundamental principles: (1) the time value of money, and (2) the level of risk that an investor is willing to accept.[2] What it does is simply to convert future values to present values so they can be used to facilitate the decision on whether the project should be funded or not. The costs are real and out-of-pocket, the future benefits are uncertain and can only be estimated. Future values are not equal to present values.

In addition to the pure time value of money expressed by the market interest rate, the risks associated with the uncertainty of the future benefits must be accounted for. If we are promised a payment of $1,000 a year from today and the market interest rate is 5 percent (the time value of money), then we would settle for a payment today of $950 to be indifferent. In other words, instead of waiting for the payment of $1,000 a year from today we would be satisfied with a payment discounted to $950 today. This is well and fine as far as it goes, but now we must add the risk factor to settle on a discount rate to reflect the college investments made by the students and taxpayers.

The selection of a discount rate adds the risk preferences involved, precisely because future cash flows are uncertain. We *think* we know what the benefits will be and specify both their magnitudes and *when* they will occur, but we don't know for sure. The risk factor is a judgment call. It depends on the nature of the investment and also on the overall investment portfolio of the investor. The state's portfolio is probably more diversified, which means the risks can be spread more so than an individual's portfolio.

In the 2014 aggregate study conducted for all community colleges in the United States, we used an average discount rate of 4.5 percent for the students, and a 1.1 percent rate for the taxpayers based on the Congressional Budget Office (CBO) forecasts made in 2014.[3] Whether those rates are too high or too low are also judgment calls, and people can certainly become vocal about the choices depending on which side of the arguments they are on—proponents or opponents.

An NPV is reflecting the present value of the net cash flows (benefits minus costs) over time, and is expressed in dollar terms. If that one number—the NPV—is equal to $0 or positive it is judged feasible, given the same discount rate. It simply means that the present value of benefits exceeds the present value of costs.

An IRR is the most difficult to understand because it is expressed as the percentage that equates the present value of the investment to $0. In other words, the IRR *solves* for the discount rate, or selects the rate that forces the present value of benefits to be just equal to the present value of costs. How does this work? Suppose the discount rate selected by the analyst is 1.1 percent—as we selected in our 2014 study taxpayer perspective for the American Association of Community Colleges (AACC). The IRR by definition is calculating its own discount rate, which is calculated at 14.3 percent.[4] Based on the 1.1 percent chosen discount rate, we now know that the investment is feasible, or attractive. Fourteen percent beats 1.1 percent any day.

This judgment that the investment is feasible and attractive, however, only holds relative to the rate chosen. If the opponents of the requested college funding do not accept the chosen discount rate of 1.1 percent but instead argue for a 7 percent rate, perhaps for good reason, the college funding would *still* be an attractive investment because 14.3 percent is still larger than 7 percent.

The discount rate of 4.5 percent selected by the analyst to reflect the student perspective is based on the federal student loan rate, and it is a selection for the student body in general. This choice, however, is an average and must be understood as such. It is only a benchmark measure that may or may not apply to individual students as they are recruited. One individual's tipping point to invest in education, or not, may be equivalent to the long-term rate of return in the stock market, say 7 percent. In other words, if the anticipated higher earnings with education does not generate an IRR exceeding 7 percent, then the education would not be worth it. If the IRR exceeds that threshold, however, then the investment in the education is deemed attractive and the student enrolls.

Another individual's personal discount rate may be entirely different, higher or lower, for different reasons. The college recruiters should keep these nuances in mind and be prepared to explain, if needed, the full range of student perspectives in the context of the discount rate chosen. For the EIS analyst, however, the problem becomes one of choosing an acceptable discount rate for the entire student body, given the different preference functions for the individual students.

THE STUDENT PERSPECTIVE

Obviously, students would like to know if their education will eventually pay off despite any idealism they might want to pursue while attending college. Idealism trumps economics whenever students chose areas of study for which the job market is very limited. The time will come, however, when students awaken to the reality of the relationship between incurring the investments of money and time for their education, and the jobs waiting for them when they exit the college. Or, their parents will prompt them into waking up to this reality. That wake-up call is essentially the *purpose* of the investment analysis component of the EIS. For the students it is important information to know that higher earnings generate returns on investment (ROIs) that exceed the average threshold values. If they don't have a clue about the marketability of their eventual degrees, or at the very least seek some sort of guidance on what their studies might actually lead to, they are destined for a dismal economic future.

Why the student-perspective analysis is included in the EIS is because economic impacts are *only generated if the students are better off when they exit the colleges than when they enter*. If they are not, employers would not perceive any productivity gain from the college education of the workers they hire and would be unwilling to pay the higher wages. The students must earn more with the education than without it to trigger a regional impact. All we do in the EIS is to confirm that, indeed, the investment is paying off for the students, *on average*.[5] It, therefore, provides context to the regional impact analysis metric based on spending, and it certainly bolsters the credibility of the higher workforce productivity claims.

This is exactly what the EIS does. With the 2,000-plus EISs completed so far, we have consistently observed the students are, indeed, far better off economically with the education received than without it, on average. This is confirmed by the investment analysis results for the students—they are considerably higher than the threshold values. For the colleges, this fact alone also becomes an effective recruiting tool.

The nuts and bolts of the student-perspective analysis are simple. We compare what the average students invest during the analysis year to the expected higher earnings per year in the future. The earnings estimate is based on career earnings functions for the occupations served by the programs offered by the college, assuming that the students, when entering the workforce, will be employed in one of those occupations. In our research over the years, at least 64 percent of the students graduating from community colleges actually work in the areas for which they were educated (outside of the students enrolled in the humanities, social sciences, general art, math, and physical sciences).[6]

The student-investment consists of tuition/fees, interest incurred on student loans, and opportunity costs. The former is out-of-pocket costs or financial aid (Pell grants, student loans, parents, or rich uncles).[7] As students take out loans, they must pay back these loans with interest over a period of time in the future. The latter is simply the wages forgone by choosing to be in school rather than be gainfully employed. Of the two, the opportunity cost is, by far, the most significant cost factor and it is carefully estimated in the Emsi EIS model. More community college students tend to be gainfully employed—full- or part-time—than most four-year university students, and that has a direct bearing on the ROI for the students. Because they tend to be more gainfully employed to provide for their families, the community college students are, on average, completing only 14 credit hour equivalents (CHEs) per year, or about half of the time of full-time students, as found in the 2014 Emsi study for all community colleges in the United States.[8]

The student perspective IRR is also measured as a weighted average for the entire student body, not for individual programs. As stated earlier, our objective is simply to confirm that students at a college, *on average*, are economically better off with their education than without it. Of course, there are large IRR variations between programs, but this level of granularity would only be required for a program-by-program analysis, not for a broader college impact analysis.

The IRR measurement for the students was found to be 17.8 percent in the 2014 study.[9] This means that for every dollar invested out-of-pocket in the forms of tuition and fees plus the interest on student loans and opportunity cost of earnings forgone for not working or only working part-time while attending the college, a 17.8 percent annual return per year is generated.

This *is* an attractive return. It certainly beats the stock market—another perceived attractive investment—where average long-term returns are only 7 percent at the time of the study. And, it beats a whole host of other investment opportunities, including the chosen discount rate of 4.5 percent. For the colleges, an average return like this can be instantly translated into a recruiting tool. It confirms that students, in general, are considerably better off investing in their education than investing elsewhere.

Another technical nuance that college presidents should know about is that the discount rate chosen *and* the percentage annual return (IRR) are quoted as *real*, as opposed to *nominal* rates of return. The nominal rate includes inflation, the real rate does not. When a bank promises to pay a certain rate of interest on a savings account, it employs an implicitly nominal rate. Bonds operate in a similar manner. If it turns out that the inflation rate is higher than the stated rate of return, then money is lost in real terms.

In contrast, a real rate of return is on top of inflation. For example, if inflation is running at 3 percent and a nominal rate of 5 percent is paid, then the real rate of return on the investment is only 2 percent. The 17.8 percent student rate of return (as in the example above) is a real rate. With an inflation rate of 2.5 percent (the average rate reported over the past 20 years as per the US Department of Commerce, Consumer Price Index), the corresponding nominal rate of return in this case would be 20.3 percent.

Apart from the standard investment analysis for the students, one distinguishing feature of the Emsi model is the application of the *Mincer function*, based on the work developed by Jacob Mincer in 1958.[10] It allowed us to *approximate the results of a true longitudinal study* based on simulated data calibrated to the earnings differentials for specific regions. Using this approach also allowed us to keep the costs per study down to a reasonable level. Longitudinal studies can be very expensive and take a lot of time. The current model, however, is even more granular and data-driven. With American Community Survey (ACS) data we now calculate a Mincer formula for every state and every education level. It is based on real data and is state- and education level-specific.

The Mincer earning function accounts for the age, educational level, and experience of the students in determining how much additional productivity gain we can add for the analysis year. In the beginning, the earnings are low relative to the earnings later when age and experience are rewarded. The earnings function has a sigmoidal shape—increasing at an increasing rate in the beginning, a point of inflection, and then increasing at a decreasing rate over time until it peaks and then begins to decline. One average Mincer function is constructed for a college's student body as a whole based on the composite of earnings in that particular region.

The earnings level in the Mincer function used in the measurement of the overall regional economic well-being begins with annual earnings at the *midpoint* of a student's career. That midpoint is derived in each study based on the age of the student body of that particular student body for the analysis year. If the retirement age is 65 and the average age of the student body is 25, the students have 40 years left in the workforce. The midpoint is at age 43. That is a static point and does not change as the student's age changes. This means at 43 years old the

Mincer is 1.0. The students' average age affects where we put them on the Mincer curve. If they are an older student body, then they probably have experience in the workforce and will be further along the Mincer curve than a student body that is just starting out at the age of 19. The average earnings are scaled in accordance with the Mincer equation used to characterize the trajectory of earnings over time.[11]

But the analytical complexities don't stop there—the trajectory of earnings over time is further adjusted downward to correct for "ability bias" and other counterfactuals discussed in previous chapters in an effort to avoid overstatement of wage benefits.[12] The ability bias is just the name given to account for the fact that correlation does not equal causation. We need to make an adjustment—scale down—the earnings that analysts can claim education generates. The so-adjusted earnings differentials may be described as indicating the *net return* to education.

This includes even a few hours of study for students who enroll simply to improve their skills or otherwise enhance their careers. If a worker takes a four-week course at a local college on the most up-to-date tractor mechanics, he becomes more proficient in a certain aspect of his occupation as a result of that training, even though no credential is awarded. The market recognizes the value of these added skills in terms of earnings differentials, which is captured and measured by the Mincer function. Of course, those returns are not as high as those that accrue to students who achieve full credentials.

THE TAXPAYER PERSPECTIVE

The investment analysis for the taxpayer perspective uses the exact same approach—i.e., the results are expressed in terms of NPVs, B/C ratios, and IRRs. The Mincer functions for the students are used since we calculate the added tax revenues based on the higher earnings of the students over their working lifetime as shown on those functions. For the taxpayers, we are measuring how much the college returns to the state treasury (through the students as they become members of the workforce) relative to the amount of taxes siphoned off to support the colleges. If the returns are higher than the amount siphoned out, then the investment is worthwhile.

The unfortunate thing is that the taxpayers don't generally think of the colleges as economic engines; they only know what they—the taxpayers—pay annually in property and state taxes. The overall perception is that the colleges are just another drain over which they have little control. The opportunity should never, therefore, be lost to the college presidents of the need to educate the taxpayers, in no uncertain terms, that community colleges indeed *are* economic engines and that they (the taxpayers) are far better off with the colleges in their midst than without them.

Higher earnings by the students as they become members of the regional workforce—a direct result of the programs offered at the college—beget added tax revenues and the present values of those benefits almost always exceed the present value of the investments made. In our experience over the years, this message has not been presented to the state and regional stakeholders as effectively as it should. The hard-earned money taxed away for supporting a nearby college generates a strong return, not just generically, but also directly back to the taxpayers.

Over the past 19 years we have conducted economic impact studies we have heard different stories from the communities. Many taxpayers still perceive a community college to be more like a black hole into which they pour their money every year, never to be seen again. This attitude is often manifested in stories appearing front and center in op-ed pieces and letters to the editors. One particular story that is always told in just about any community is the one that laments the college's exemption from property taxes. They, therefore, cost the taxpayers through tax revenues forgone.

Added to the cost of the tax appropriations and property tax levies, the taxpayers are far too often left with the perception that the college is a burden, not an economic blessing. Over the past 19 years, we have worked hard to change this perception using the meaning of the EIS results effectively, and that includes a much stronger emphasis placed on the economic *benefits* of having the college there.[13]

The return from the taxpayers' perspective is measured two ways: the "social" and the "taxpayer" ROI.

Social: The Broad Perspective

Generally, the role of government is to provide services that the public wants, but the business sector finds unprofitable. The costs are borne by the taxpayers, but the benefits are widely dispersed. In the broad perspective, we look at the taxpayer investment in the college the same way as we look at any other public investment, like building a state highway or establishing a state park. Both are examples of investments that must be public, i.e., using taxpayer money. Building highways or creating state parks are necessary goods the public wants, but they do not attract private investors because the investors (the taxpayers) and the beneficiaries are not one and the same, and the benefits are widely dispersed.

A new state highway, for example, benefits the motorists who are safer, consume less gas, and save time in traveling from point A to point B. There is no direct linkage between those who invest (the taxpayers) and those who benefit (the motorists) since not all motorists on the state highway are the state's taxpayers.

Or, alternatively, the creation of a state park will justify the use of public funds by showing that recreation values accruing to park users, plus the benefits accruing to local businesses, exceed the public outlay for park creation and operation. Again, the beneficiaries are widely dispersed. *All* of the benefits are tallied up, not just those that accrue back to the government, and measured against the costs incurred by the investors.

For any public investment schemes such as these, all economists must do is to demonstrate that the present value of the benefits, *to whomever they accrue*, must equal or exceed present value of all the costs incurred. If so, the investment is deemed feasible. This is the meaning and method of broad perspective return-on-investment analyses. The attractiveness of such expenditures is expressed through the use of a B/C ratio where a ratio equal to or greater than one is minimally necessary for a worthwhile public project and an NPV, where if it is greater than 0, is deemed a worthwhile investment.

A community college too is a public investment. The investments in the college should be measured against the returns they generate back to the investors. Since it is a public investment, however, it is analyzed as such—most of the costs are borne by the taxpayers. The benefits, on the other hand, are the higher earnings accrued by the students. Not one and the same—the taxpayers are not directly reaping the benefits.

The results from the many EISs we have conducted over the past 19 years reveal that the costs are almost always exceeded manyfold by the benefits (the higher earnings received by the students). In addition, we add in the *external* benefits. Recall from earlier discussions, these include savings in the healthcare budget, reduced expenditures on crime (e.g., prosecution, incarceration, and victim costs), and reduced expenses on welfare and unemployment expenditures. These benefits accrue to different publics (students, employers, victims of crime, the federal government, *and* state and local taxpayers). Because of these typically large benefits relative to the low costs accrued by different publics, we fully expect a high B/C ratio. And this has been our experience.

In the 2014 aggregate (nationwide) study we conducted for AACC, we measured a B/C ratio of 25.9, or the benefits exceeded costs by a factor of nearly 26.[14] Included in that measurement were the benefits from 11.6 million credit students served, earning 163 million credit hours (14 CHEs earned on average per year), which generated an expanded economic base plus savings related to improved health, reduced crime, and reduced unemployment by a present value of $1.2 trillion. The present value of the aggregate costs (the investments) that generated this benefit stream was the comparatively smaller amount—nearly $45 billion. The NPV, therefore, was $1.1 trillion—a very attractive public investment.[15]

Taxpayer: The Narrow Perspective

But, the (narrow) taxpayer perspective is by far the most interesting story, the most revealing one, and the one most untold story (until the Emsi study came along). From this perspective, the public investment is treated *as if it were a private investment* where the investors and the beneficiaries are one and the same. This means we must identify a subset of the benefits stream in the social perspective that accrue directly and only back to the taxpayers (the investors). Public investments, as defined, rarely generate a positive return *from the investors' perspectives*, which is precisely why we have public investments such as national or state parks, public transportation, police departments, and the like.

So, to define the subset of benefits accrued by the taxpayers, we need to summarize where we are thus far. The taxpayers invest in the forms of state tax appropriations (and/or property taxes) to support the colleges. The *taxpayers pay* and the *students benefit* through higher earnings. Thus far, there is no obvious and direct linkage between those who invest and those who receive the benefits.

Now suppose the students earn, on average, a net of $3,000 more per year (after having made all of the counterfactual adjustments) because of the education received. After multiplying this by the number of students and deducting the costs of providing the education, we arrive at a measure of the college's net influence on student earnings. If the present value of the benefits (higher earnings) is equal to or greater than the present value of the costs, then we deem the college's operation to be feasible, and attractive. This is a summary of the social (broader) perspective.

For the community colleges, defining the subset of benefits is actually a simple process. Out of the $3,000 increase in average earnings per student (multiplied by the number of students) there will also be an average increase in *tax collections*. That *is* the subset. Suppose for every $3,000 increase in earnings, the state sees an increase in average tax collections of $300 per student (again, multiplied by the number of students), for a total benefit stream that replenishes the state treasury. Counting only the tax collections as benefits will make the investors (the taxpayers), and the beneficiaries (the taxpayers) one and the same.

If the aggregate increase in *tax collections* equal or exceed the costs of providing the education (i.e., the state appropriations and/or the property taxes portion used to support the college), then the college can claim responsibility for putting at least as much money back into the treasury as it takes out. In addition to this, we also determine the added tax collections from the spending impacts that occur because of the college, which broadens the tax base.

In fact, in the vast majority of studies completed, the community colleges are responsible for replenishing the state treasury based on higher tax collections much more than they take out in the forms of state appropriations and local property taxes. In the nationwide aggregate study, we measured the IRR at 14.3 percent, far above the threshold value.[16] This is the biggest untold, or poorly told, story out there.

Given great results such as these, the taxpayers should be told time and again that property taxes would probably increase were it not for the presence of the publicly funded colleges in the region. Or, tell the story differently. Were it not for the additional tax collections from the higher earnings made possible by the education provided, the state budget would be tighter and either state services would either have to be reduced, or taxes would have to increase to maintain services at current levels. The community college performs a great economic service to the region's taxpayers by its presence in the region, and in doing what it does—educating people. By virtue of that education, they earn more, pay more in taxes, and incur budgetary savings for the state because they behave better socially (less crime, less welfare and unemployment, and improved health habits).

So, to summarize—when the (narrow) returns to the taxpayers exceed threshold levels, one can conclude that the college *subsidizes* the taxpayer-provided services in each state to a significant extent. When these (investment) conditions are met, the students and taxpayers are better off economically with the college and the education it provides than without it.

WHO BENEFITS MORE: THE STUDENTS OR THE PUBLIC?

Now, having briefly discussed the differences between the broad and narrow taxpayer perspectives and why they are important, we have at least shed some light on the lingering perception of why the taxpayers should support community college education at all. Reducing or even eliminating public support for education is still argued for by a significant portion of the population on the grounds that *students* clearly capture the benefits of higher education, and so they should be asked to bear the bulk (perhaps all) of the costs. At least so it seems at a first glance.

On the surface of it, these are not unreasonable arguments. There is definitely a limit to how much the public should support education. In our opinion, community college education should not be free (see chapter 5), nor should it be entirely unsupported. There is an optimal level of funding to be defined, although that level will remain undefined, at least for purposes of this book. Suffice it to say, however, that the level of public support of community colleges is definitely an artful balancing act.

For now, the EIS results and the due diligence they can bring to bear on this quandary of who benefits the most, *is* the context. The EIS results *can,* in many cases, tell the story that community college education in many cases actually benefits the public more than the students, as illustrated (hypothetically) in table 3.1.

The values in the top two rows refer to the students; the other rows refer to the public benefits. The first column in the table shows the benefits amounting to, in this particular case, $200 per CHE in the form of higher earnings, after having adjusted for all the counterfactuals. The second column shows the same benefits per full-time student assuming that the average CHE accomplishment during the analysis year was 11 credit hours per student.

As shown in the table, the average student will see his or her gross annual earnings increase by $200 for every CHE of instruction completed. Monies paid in taxes do not directly benefit the student as such, but rather the taxpaying public, so the appropriate figure for judging student benefits is increased earnings *after tax.* The $175 per CHE shown in the second row of the table is the benefit per CHE net of the combined federal, state, and local taxes, or $1,925 per full-time student.

The public, however, also benefits from higher workforce productivity based on the fact that regional employers pay more for workers with education than without. This means that more educated, more productive, and higher earnings recipients buy better houses and newer and better cars, replace their appliances more frequently, and so on. The workforce improves in both quality and quantity, and gross state product (GSP) gradually rises as a result. This measure is often higher per CHE than the benefits accrued to the students for two reasons: (1) the

Table 3.1. Student vs. Public Benefits

Student Benefits	Per CHE ($)	Per FT Student ($)
Increased student earnings, gross	200	2,200
Increased student earnings, after tax	175	1,925
Public Benefits		
Increased GRP	225	2.475
Externalities (cost savings)	10	110
Total public benefits	235	2,585

agglomeration of the added regional workforce productivity, and (2) the transfer payments to the workers over time (investments returns, IRAs, and such). This amounts to a total of $225 per CHE in this example, or $2,475 per full-time student.

In addition to the public benefits, we have the assortment of externalities (or avoided public costs) associated with reduced unemployment and welfare, improved health habits, and reduced crime, etc., which adds a total of $10 per CHE as shown in the next to the last row in the table, or $110 per full-time student. These are counted as well because they include the savings to the state every year attributable to improved social behavior. There will be less crime, improved health (less smoking and alcohol abuse), lower expenditures on unemployment and welfare, etc. as education levels increase.

State and local governments bear part of the costs of poor social behaviors, and so their budgets benefit from education-induced reductions of these behaviors in the form of avoided costs. The bottom line: while state and local governments spend money in support of the colleges, they also receive benefits in the form of an assortment of avoided costs.

In the row "Total public benefits" we show that the public benefits, *in this case*, by roughly $1.34 per $1.00 of net student benefits ($235 / $175 = $1.34), or significantly higher than shown for the students. (Per full-time student, the corresponding numbers are $2,585/$1,925= $1.34.)

THE REDUNDANT SEMESTER

There is another, albeit "smaller," issue that the EIS results can help resolve—the negative economic impact that deficient articulation agreements between community colleges and the universities might have on the region. Taxpayers should know and understand this, and it is the college presidents' responsibility to tell this story as well, and with numbers. If an existing articulation agreement is *not* paving the way for smooth transitions between colleges and universities, then negative economic consequences will unfold, and *that* is important for the taxpayers to know so that they, in turn, can be energized in their support of the colleges.

A deficient agreement is when community college students do not receive full credit for their studies at a community college when transferring to four-year universities. Three calculus credits earned at a community college, for example, do not always transfer as three credits of calculus at a four-year university, even if the same textbooks are used. Indeed, as most community college leaders will agree, there is a tendency to undervalue community college credits earned relative to similar credits earned at four-year universities.

Obviously, if community college education adequately prepares students for further education at four-year universities, then the articulation agreement should reflect so, otherwise it needs to be fixed. Any fractional transfer value of community college credits earned becomes a redundancy in education that, in turn, translates into a direct and measurable lost economic value that can be estimated, but only if the EIS results and databases are available. What is the true cost to the student and to society at large of one semester where students are obliged to repeat courses at the four-year university that they have already completed at the community college? At best, that semester can be labeled *redundant*.

When transfer students have to repeat courses at the four-year university, they and society both incur economic losses. Not only do the students pay twice for the same courses, they also delay their entry into the workforce to become productive members. These are costs borne by the students and society at large, and particularly by the taxpayers since they fund *both* the college and the university.

The analysis is anchored to a standard full-time semester, i.e., 15 credit hours or CHEs. For purposes of this analysis, we assume that the student will have had to repeat a full semester's worth of study by the time he or she transfers to a four-year university (redundancy cost estimates can be scaled up or down in a linear fashion depending on the actual credit hours repeated).

To calculate the cost of the redundancies, we extract the following measures from the impact study databases:

- The student costs, composed of the opportunity cost of time (the value of time the students give up while attending college instead of working) and the tuition and fee payments;

- the private-sector investments—monies from private donors and private contract-funded courses; and
- the public-sector investments—state and local government funding, plus Pell grants and other aid.

We put this (hypothetical) data together to derive an estimate of the cost of a repeated semester at the university, as presented in table 3.2.

As shown in the table, the estimated total cost of a redundant semester for one student is $9,400. The largest portion of this cost is $5,500, or 59 percent of the total, borne by the students in the form of wages forgone while attending. The students could have entered the workforce earlier instead of having to spend the extra time to repeat courses at the four-year university. Not counted here are the additional taxes that *could* have been collected on the $5,500 if the students had entered the workforce earlier instead of repeating the courses.

Tuition is the second item of cost shown in the table. The tuition cost of a full-time semester amounts to $850, or 9 percent of the total cost. These two items—the $5,500 plus $850—amounts to 68 percent of the total cost of a full-time semester at this particular college, on average. It indicates that the student bears by far the largest share of the cost of a redundant semester.

The next item in the table is labeled "Private (employer) support," or the monies provided by the private sector through donations and earmarked training—employer-funded community college education for short. This amounts to $400, or 4 percent of the total cost. The state and local government subsidy amounts to another $2,200, or 23 percent of total costs. The last item, $450, or 5 percent of all costs, is borne by the federal government in the form of Pell grants and other federal aid.

Table 3.2. Cost per Student

Cost per Student (Sources)	Total ($)	%
Student opportunity cost of time	5,500	59
Student tuition	850	9
Private (employer) support	400	4
State support (state and local govt.)	2,200	23
Federal support (Pell and other grants)	450	5
Total	9,400	100

All told, the failure to operate under optimal articulation agreements leads to losses amounting to an estimated average of $9,400 per semester, per student, borne by the students themselves, the local and state taxpayers, and the federal government.

These losses are eminently avoidable if the education establishment in the state were to focus on ensuring that the transition from a community college to a four-year university is virtually seamless. This would mean that the community colleges and the universities in the state meet regularly to explicitly define the parameters of their transfer programs and policies.

GROWTH VS. IMPACTS

Finally, an EIS is also about economic growth and not only about impacts. They are not synonymous terms. Think of a sink filling with water as in figure 3.1. *Growth* occurs if the amount of water coming from the faucet exceeds the amount of water lost through the drain over time. The water level rises. The *impact* is the difference in the level of water in the sink brought before and after the set period of inflow and outflow. *Pouring* the water into the sink is the impact. It can be negative if the outflow exceeds the inflow, and positive in the reverse case.

Switching the analogy to the community colleges—if the CHEs entering the economy through the workforce during the analysis year exceed the number of CHEs exiting on the other end of the spectrum due to the alumni out-migrating, retiring, and dying, then we have growth. In other words, the water level in the sink is slightly higher than it was last year, and we have a measurable impact. If the leakages (again, due to out-migration, retirement, or death) exceed the CHEs injected into the workforce, then we have measurable decline, or negative impact. If the inflow is equal to the outflow, the impact is zero.

The *cumulative* number of CHEs embedded in the regional workforce still adding value in the regional workforce at a given point in time is represented by the water level itself at a given point in time. If the college were to shut down, it would have the same effect as turning off the faucet. The regional impacts would turn negative and slowly dissipate over time as retirement, out-migration, and death outpace a zero inflow of new students, so economic growth would immediately cease.

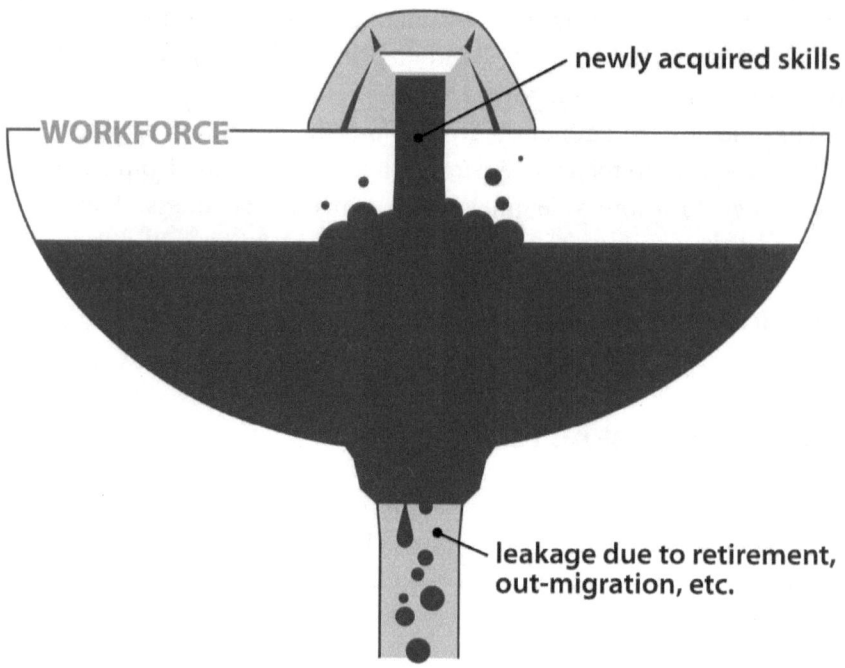

Figure 3.1. Growth vs. impact

The regional impact does not only derive from increasing the number of CHEs relative to the leakages out of the economy, which is why impact metrics sometimes vary counterintuitively. How can you have a low impact if the number of CHEs embedded in the workforce increased? This is counterintuitive, to put it mildly. There may still be some impact (the water level has risen), but not commensurate with the disproportional increase in CHEs.

The impact is also dependent on what else is happening in the region, which is out of the control of the colleges. Suppose the EIS results from a study conducted two years ago are still fresh in the minds of all the stakeholders. They were used many times to great effect, the impacts were impressive, and they were derived correctly—i.e., having adjusted for all the counterfactuals to present net, not gross numbers.

Now, two years later, the *new* impact study comes in with lower impact results—say a full 15 percent lower—the water level in the sink has failed to increase commensurately. At this point, the college president and governing board would rightfully be taken by an unpleasant surprise because the student headcount increased substantially over the two years, and so the impact should be a lot higher. Nobody expects lower regional impacts, so when the new results show a decreased regional impact compared to a previous study, how can this be?

The simple answer is that other variables are at play over which the college has not control, variables that can more than offset the gains in impact from student growth with larger losses elsewhere. One of the explanations could be what may have happened to the economic base—the economic underpinnings of the region—over the past two years. If the economic base remained unchanged over the years (meaning the players are roughly the same and their economic performance did not vary much), we *should* register an increasing impact over the two years if the college had increased the number of students served, all else being equal.

But we didn't.

All else is rarely equal. Perhaps during that time some large companies uprooted and left, i.e., the leakages are greater than the inflows and/or the multiplier becomes smaller. This happens all over the country, and such events will certainly reduce the total impact in dollar terms because now there are fewer employment opportunities, so the leavers from the college seek employment outside the region. Or, the economy may have slowed significantly. Any increased impact attributable to *more* students enrolled may be more than offset by other changes in the regional economy. There can be many reasons that presidents and governing boards need to understand the regional economy and the major variables at play. The EIS results and databases are a very good place to start.

CONCLUSION

We have now highlighted what the investment analysis component of an EIS is and provided the proper context for the results via a discussion of the benchmark numbers, or the threshold values to which the results could be compared to give them meaning. If the results exceed the threshold values, college presidents can take comfort in the knowledge that the results are attractive compared to many other investment alternatives. If not, perhaps next year we should invest in different things.

The investment component of the impact study is essentially a "luxury" that only enriches the measures of the dollar impact the colleges have on the regions they serve. It provides needed context to the economic impact results. Every community college has an economic impact on its region simply by virtue of its existence. The context provided by the investment analysis results is to show whether the money invested by the students generates a return to them that makes it worthwhile to enroll. Many times the results show that students investing in their education is superior to alternative investment opportunities.

Likewise, taxpayers can take comfort in the results from their perspective if the results exceed the threshold values. For most studies we have conducted over the years, not only do the investments in the community colleges generally pay off as both *public* and *private* investments. The former is where the present value of benefits exceeds the present value of the costs, *regardless of to whom the benefits may accrue*. The latter is when the investment is regarded just like private investments *when the investors and beneficiaries are one and the same*. The difference between a public and private investment is that the taxpayers bear the brunt of the costs for both, but the beneficiaries are different. The students receive the *higher earnings* in the public investment. The taxpayers receive only the *added tax revenues* from those higher earnings in the same analysis but viewed as a private investment analysis.

Finally, we concluded the chapter with brief discussions of three topics: who benefits from higher education more—the students or the public; the cost of a redundant semester when articulation agreements between colleges and universities are deficient; and the nuances of the terms "economic impacts" and "economic growth."

The availability of the EIS results can shed light on the first and second topics. Education is one of those unique investment opportunities that have both private and public benefits. On the private side, the students are the primary beneficiaries because they enjoy the higher earnings attributable to the education they receive. But the public generally benefits more. Because the students have higher earnings, they also pay more in taxes, and employers enjoy the fruits of the education because the workforce is now more productive. This, in turn, means that the economy is improving both quantitatively and qualitatively, people buy better houses and drive better and newer cars, etc. Do the math. When added up, the public actually benefits more than the higher earnings enjoyed by the students.

Having students repeat courses at the university that they successfully completed at the community colleges can be quite costly. If the articulation agreements between the colleges and universities are deficient, then costs of redundancies become real. A redundancy delays the onset of higher earnings by the students, and the public sees a delay in the onset of higher workforce productivity.

These two—the fact that the public may benefit more, and the economic costs of a redundant semester—are also reasons why a college should commission an EIS more frequently than the current average of every three to four years. The regional data used in the analysis will sometimes change drastically in even one year. Lots can happen in one year, and relying on impact results with stale data can be counterproductive.

Finally, the economic impact on a region is measured for the analysis year—it is a static measure based on the snapshot of data collected for the college and the region. The college will always have an impact, but economic growth can sometimes be elusive. They are not always moving in the same direction.

NOTES

1. In addition, we also include a payback period measure—how many years it takes for the original investment to be paid off. This, however, is not a "time value of money" kind of measure. Note that the IRR is one of the metrics we measure, which should not be confused with an ROI (although many do). The ROI is technically just the B/C ratio minus 1×100 (a pretty straightforward formula). IRR is a useful measure on its own, but it is especially useful when compared to other investment options, such as the stock market.

2. Economic Modeling Specialists International, *Demonstrating the Value of America's Community Colleges, Analysis of the Economic Impact and Return on Investment of Education*, January 2014.

3. Ibid.

4. Ibid.

5. "On average" means that some students will never earn back the investments made—the programs chosen do not lead to any gainful employment. On the other side of the bell curve, however, some programs lead to much higher-than-average earning occupations.

6. Emsi Alumni Outcome software

7. A grant *in excess of the cost* of tuition, of course, is not a cost in the model, it is a benefit. For the sake of simplicity, we assume that the Pell grants, or student loans, are indeed reflecting costs only.

8. Economic Modeling Specialists International, *Demonstrating the Value of America's Community Colleges*, 12.

9. Ibid.

10. Jacob Mincer, "Investment in Human Capital and Personal Income Distribution," *Journal of Political Economy* 66, no. 4 (August 1958): 281–302. We obtained our precalibrated Mincer function from R. J. Willis, *Handbook of Labor Economics*, vol. 1 (Amsterdam: North-Holland Press, 2001), chap. 10.

11. While some have criticized Mincer's earnings function, it is still upheld in recent data and has served as the foundation for a variety of research pertaining to labor economics. Those critical of the Mincer function point to several unobserved factors such as ability, socioeconomic status, and family background that also help explain higher earnings. Failure to account for these factors results in what is known as an "ability bias," a counterfactual that we include in our model.

12. The adjustments are directed by G. S. Becker, *Human Capital: A Theoretical and Empirical Analysis, with Special Reference to Education* (New York: Columbia College Press for NBER, 1993). (See "Ability" in the Subject Index.)

13. An effective reply to the property taxes forgone argument (and to step away from the investment analysis for just a moment) is that students from outside the region spend new money in the region—money that would not otherwise be spent there. The money spent by them alone, in the vast majority of cases, would offset any lost property-tax revenues many times over. In addition to that, the added regional earnings and tax collections from students as they enter the workforce make the property tax revenues lost insignificant.

14. Economic Modeling Specialists International, *Demonstrating the Value of America's Community Colleges*. Note that this measurement was done using Emsi's old methodology of counting only the taxpayer costs. Today, that methodology has changed to include all college expenditures and student costs.

15. Ibid.

16. Ibid.

4

WHAT AN EIS IS NOT—DEALING WITH THE "SHORTCOMINGS"

Production Possibilities Frontier

In this chapter we look at what an economic impact study (EIS) is not, its limits or shortcomings, and how to deal with them. To set the stage, we begin with the broadest shortcoming: the EIS does not measure if a college allocates its resources optimally, or even efficiently. It measures what *is*, not what *ought to be*. We introduced the concept of an optimal allocation of fixed resources among alternative and competing ends in earlier chapters. Now we look into this concept a little deeper by presenting a short primer on the production possibilities frontier, a theoretical construct in economics that makes it easier to understand the idea of an optimal allocation of resources.[1]

A college can only do so much given a fixed annual budget. It can focus on placing students in jobs (job placement), or producing credit hours (student retention), widely different and broad objectives that both have political opponents and proponents. These objectives are mutually exclusive for purposes of our discussion. If the college devotes the bulk of its resources to guide students toward job placements, that objective could be successfully achieved only at the expense of devoting fewer resources to retaining students. Or, vice versa. The objectives are different and require different management strategies, and they have different political consequences.

There is an imaginary *production possibilities frontier* out there that marks the optimal and most efficient allocation of resources possible, as depicted in figure 4.1. The objective is to get as close to that frontier as possible. To be on the frontier, as shown by colleges 1 and 2, would mean that their respective resources (the budgets) are allocated optimally, given their chosen strategies (i.e., maximizing placements or retention). In other words, these colleges could not allocate them any more efficiently.

Any location on the frontier—from point A to point B—is consistent with an optimal allocation of resources. That means the colleges would buy their supplies from the most competitive vendors, there would be an optimal mix of adjunct vs. permanent faculty, the student body served would be of perfect size, the faculty/student ratio would be just right, and so on. The only real challenge would be the choice of leaning toward one of the two broad objectives because it would trigger different managerial, political, and economic outcomes.

The specific location on the frontier—closer to A or B—would reflect managerial *and* political decisions made by the college leadership. If all of the resources were devoted to student job placements, it would be reflected by point A. All the resources devoted to retaining the

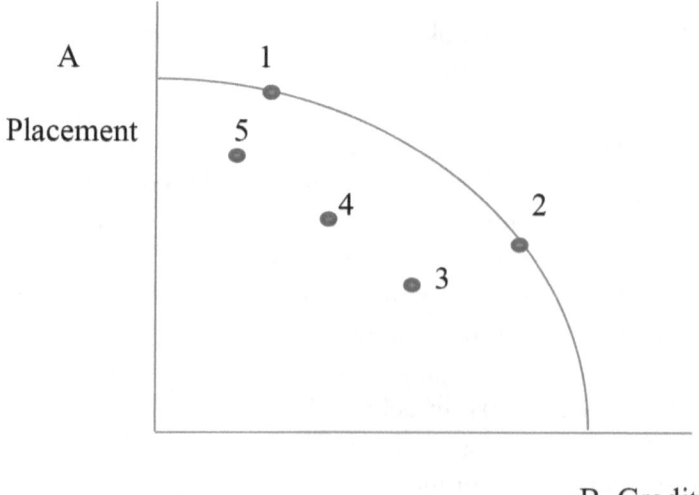

Figure 4.1. Employment vs. retention

students to maximize the credit production are reflected by point B. Any point along the A to B production possibilities frontier reflects an emphasis *toward* A or *toward* B—a combined allocation of resources—but still most efficient allocation possible.

Colleges 1 and 2 are probably fictitious. At least this has been our experience so far. No college, as far as we know, has earned the distinction of having allocated resources perfectly. Most colleges operate well below the frontier (e.g., colleges 3, 4, and 5) and have a long way to go before they reach optimal resource allocation. Some are closer than others, but the fact remains, resources in most cases could be allocated much more efficiently.

Perhaps the winners of the Aspen Prize could be identified as coming closest to being on the frontier, although the selection process is not necessarily based on efficiency principles on economic theory:

> To award the Aspen Prize for Community College Excellence, the College Excellence Program engages in a rigorous two-year-long process that assesses student outcomes at over 1,000 community colleges in the United States, leading to the selection of ten finalists and, ultimately, one winner. Institutions are assessed for exceptional student outcomes in four areas: student learning, certificate and degree completion (including of a bachelor's degree after transfer), employment and earnings, and high levels of access and success for minority and low-income students. Throughout the process, Aspen looks extensively at data, engages community college leaders, and solicits guidance from experts in higher education.[2]

The Aspen Prize is awarded to one community college each year, after which they become beacons of colleges to emulate. Winning this prize should always be the quest of individual colleges, although it does not define whether resources are optimally allocated.

The difference in the placement inside the frontier of colleges 3, 4, and 5 is a reflection of the strategic choices made by the college leadership in how the fixed resources should be managed throughout the year. These colleges are on different trajectories, and each trajectory has real political consequences. College 5 is much more focused on the need to place students in jobs and maintain a program mix to support this than college 3. College 3 chose to devote relatively more resources to the production of credits (i.e., the retention objective) and maintains a different program mix more conducive to this strategy. College 4 is in the middle of the road.

The different strategies may all generate stellar EIS results. But that is not enough. The due diligence must still be made to assess the political consequences of choosing which strategy to implement. There are tradeoffs. These can be measured by the extent to which the regional economic activities will be affected up or down as a result of the strategies tested. If a strategy leaning toward job placements (A) leads to a higher gross regional product (GRP) than a strategy leaning toward credit production (B), the economic difference between the two is the cost of choosing B over A. This, of course, is not to say that choosing A over B (or B over A) will always be the right choice. It is to say that college presidents need to know and be able to communicate why leaning toward A or B might still be the better choice for reasons other than economic ones, particularly when meeting with legislators and other stakeholders.

Suppose a college offers a particular program mix with a strong focus on credit production and retention with the following EIS results: net regional impact of $400 million per year, a taxpayer (narrow perspective) return of investment (ROI) of 12 percent, and a student ROI of 13 percent. All solid EIS results. Both taxpayer and student ROI results are well above threshold levels.

If, for whatever reason, the political winds change, the college leadership may become convinced that a much stronger focus on job placements is vitally necessary for next year. The means of achieving this change in direction is to alter the program mix. Suppose further that the college conducted a "what-if" analysis using the EIS databases with the following results: a changed program mix reveals that the annual regional economic impact would change to $405 million per year, a $5 million increase, all else being equal. The $5 million increase in the GRP would certainly resonate with the taxpayers (and the legislators).

The taxpayer (narrow perspective) and student ROIs, however, would reduce to 10 percent and 12 percent, respectively. These slightly lower results would put a bit of a damper on the enthusiasm. So, it's decision time. Should we change the program mix and thus increase the GRP next year, or should we not? And if not, why not? If we choose to continue to offer the current program mix, we now know that we will forgo a potential $5 million worth of potential GRP growth increase. That is the magnitude of the tradeoff.

An increase in the GRP is not the only consideration for changing the program mix. That much is clear. The other factors are the ROIs for the students and the taxpayers. If the ROIs drop as a result of the changes, this will weigh against the decision to change the program mix. The question, therefore, is: is the gain in the GRP *more significant* than the pain of enduring a drop in the student and taxpayer ROIs? On the investment side, the *current* program mix renders the taxpayers and students marginally better off. And, it produces more credits because more students will remain in school. These blunt another highly sensitive political issue in the education world—the student retention rate.

The solution, in our humble opinion, is to favor the change in the program mix because it actually increases the regional economic impact. Even though the investment analysis results went down a little because of the change, they are still well above the threshold values. This fact alone should render the damper on the enthusiasm insignificant, and the changes in the program mix should be made. The changes only become a problem if they trigger a drop in the ROI for either the taxpayers or the students below the threshold level.

The important point of all this is that, through this process, we will have isolated the data-driven reasons for making the change, or not making it. Those reasons can then be turned into powerful arguments for or against any changes in the current program mix. Forgoing the GRP growth may still be the most prudent decision for *noneconomic reasons*—it is important, however, that college presidents *know what those reasons are* and be able to communicate them convincingly to the stakeholders.

This exercise illustrates the usefulness of having EIS results available to justify funding requests. In the process of making choices, a college president can frame them in terms that describe the extent to which the EIS results are likely to be affected. When a college chooses one particular trajectory over another, costs and political consequences unfold. The tradeoffs between the different trajectories can be measured and invoked as arguments for or against a particular course of action.

All of this begs the question: why are these kinds of analyses already not included in the EIS? The simple answers are *cost* and *practicality*. The costs would increase if the model must always accommodate political issues that change from one year to the next (remedial training, low graduation rates, high default rates on student loans, etc.). Besides, these kinds of issues (which vary in importance between the states) are outside the boundaries of an economic impact study. It would be impractical, if not impossible, to include them all in the EIS methodology, and so, they need to be addressed separately in submodels using the EIS databases.

As discussed previously, the EIS only provides information on the impacts generated through spending and investing measured against the backdrop of a defined region of influence, regardless of how inefficiently (or efficiently) the scarce resources may have been allocated. Not included in a standard EIS, therefore, is to analyze how the results might change if inefficiencies were removed.

How the results might change if resources were allocated more efficiently is the second step. We have done the EIS and have generated the results for the snapshot of the analysis year. They are good and strong and disseminated to an appreciating audience of stakeholders. But also . . . we now have a much better feel for what we *could* have done differently to allocate resources more efficiently. We have access to the model, the most recent college and regional databases, and so the next step is to use these to simulate how the EIS results *would* have changed had we done things differently than what we actually did. That is the "what-if" analysis—the next step to be taken in preparation for next year.

Once the EIS is done, the first step toward removing the inefficiencies in how resources are internally allocated is complete. Using the EIS results in submodels as a platform to initiate the planning for the following year is the next step. Of course, there are many moving variables depending upon each other in this step that may seem overwhelming. But the availability of the EIS results, model, and databases is a huge advantage, and a "what-if" analysis need not be as sophisticated as some academicians may require. If we had tweaked program A, or replaced program A with program B at the beginning of the analysis year, how would the results likely change? Making some realistic and transparent assumptions about the behavior of key moving variables (numbers of students, dropout and retention rates, job prospects, earnings, etc.) as a result of such program changes would provide sufficiently robust answers to that question.

THE LIMITS OF THE EIS

Chapters 2 and 3 provided a detailed analysis of what an economic impact analysis for colleges is—including the all-important distinction between gross vs. net impact measures. In this chapter, we broadly discuss what an EIS is not and, more precisely, its limits. Obviously, a president *should* have a clear notion of how the presence of the college affects the regional economy. Does it increase the GRP, or detract from it, and by how much? How much of the GRP does the college account for, or explain, and why is this important to know? And, on the investment side, how do the students and taxpayers benefit from the services the college provides? Are they better or worse off? These are all important measures, and they do provide a lot of information on the college's role as a regional economic player.

Even though the EIS results are necessary, they are not sufficient. For example, they do not provide evidence of effective management of the colleges. The simple answer to that quandary is that education pays as we have measured over the past 19 years, and all we do is add the precise measurements of how well it pays. Even poorly managed colleges can demonstrate strong EIS results based on the snapshot of data used for the analysis, and if these colleges were to improve the management effectiveness, chances are that the EIS results would improve also.

But that can only be measured the next time the EIS is conducted, at which time the data snapshots would also be entirely different. Any measured improvement in the results could be attributable to the changes in the college and regional data, or changes in the effectiveness of the management, or both. In addition, the model itself is also "fluid" in the sense that the literature informs us if and when we have to make changes to it. Our obligation is to stay on top of new research and change the model parameters and functional relationships from one year to the next as needed.

The EIS results should always reflect the latest state-of-the-art assembly of functional relationship between variables possible. For these reasons, one cannot easily compare the EIS results between years.[3] If colleges do compare (and most still do despite the caveats), they should be aware of the changes in the results attributable to any modeling or background data changes that took place during the time between the studies. Obviously, the longer the period between the studies, the less meaningful any comparison will be.

Over the past 19 years of conducting the economic impact analyses for colleges, we have found the results to be strong and positive for most of them. But this does not provide political cover for the many other economic issues that college presidents must deal with daily, such as chronic budget shortfalls, low graduation rates, high default rates on student loans, "free" community colleges, enrollment woes (too high or too low), and many more. Obviously, EIS metrics cannot compensate for or solve these political and economic issues, but they are a very important first step, or baseline for demonstrating value. They are necessary, but not sufficient.

Every institution of higher education considers as its primary determinant of success the *product* the colleges produce—the collective achievement of its students. For this metric, however, on top of the success ladder for most colleges are the graduation statistics and the retention rates, not where the students end up working and changes in their earnings. Only on the lower rungs of the success ladder do we find attention to this phenomenon. The prestigious universities can get away with this, because they are . . . well . . . prestigious. But the community colleges can't. They need to put the economic impacts on top because that's where the political arena is and where the battles are fought. The headlines are all over the place lamenting the gaps between the shortcomings of the education offered at the colleges and the skill requirements for the jobs in the workforce.

Policymakers, however, often erred by treating all higher-education institutions alike. They instituted policies on graduation and retention rates through ranking scorecards that community colleges cannot live up to, *nor should*, for reasons laid out elsewhere in this book. By way of this political reality, the community colleges somehow got penalized for their typically low ranking in the budgeting process.

This perverse incentive invariably takes hold over time as community colleges have little choice but to embrace the policies and thus become more like the universities. This is the very reason why community college leaders should showcase the *economic* benefits of their activities much more aggressively as a counter to the current political trends of bowing at the altar of higher graduation and retention rates.

Slowly but surely the political winds will change, and the niches fulfilled by the community colleges will become increasingly known and accepted by policymakers and other stakeholders. To make this happen, however, community college leaders must become better at communicating the colleges' unique capabilities of increasing the GRP more so than meeting graduation and retention goals only. Fortunately, the federal government has recently committed to improving the College Scorecard by adding dimensions that the EIS provides, or potentially provides.

So, after this minor digression—back to what the EIS is not. As mentioned in the previous chapters, the impacts stemming from the college's *spending* is only the icing on the cake. The real impacts come from the education supplied and the higher earnings the students receive when they exit. This is not reflecting the higher earnings for only the analysis year, but cumulatively throughout their entire careers. Our task as analysts is to measure the dollars-and-cents value of that education.

Observed vs. Optimal Behavior

In the EIS we take as a given the college's decisions about how the factors of production (faculty and staff, infrastructure, program mix, etc.) *are* combined, not on how the college *should* have combined them. We base our analysis on *observed* behavior, not *optimal* behavior. So, if this year's combination of the factors of production is deficient—or somewhere less than optimal—then changing it for the next year would be an improvement. This applies not only to the economic impacts themselves, but also to other political and economic issues.

Note here that *"changing it for the next year would be an improvement"* refers only to what the "what-if" analysis shows. The changes contemplated are entered into the model as if we began the analysis year with those changes, holding everything else equal, and then the analysis would be rerun to determine if the results would change.

Changing the program mix, for example, could trigger a drop in the default rate on student loans, which in turn, would generate corresponding changes in the EIS results. The college president, therefore, should use the EIS results as the connector of all dots—the common denominator—in addressing multivariate issues. Therein lays the major value of the EIS. It should never be regarded as a mere separable activity—a box the college presidents can simply check as the year progresses.

Information vs. Recommendations

The EIS, as the model is currently structured, is an analytical tool *with limits*. To be well acquainted with those limits is very important because it prevents the college leadership from presenting the results out of context. The main limit is that it only provides vital *information* in the form of impact metrics; it does not make *recommendations*. Ideally, the former should inform the latter.

So, here's the problem. If only half of the equation—the information—is presented to the stakeholders, and the other half—the recommendations—is not, this becomes an opportunity lost. The opportunity is simply to use the EIS results as a platform to make recommendations on strategies intended to resolve other issues (this will be covered in greater detail in chapter 6). The common denominator becomes the extent to which the GRP changes when any of the strategies are implemented, and that can only be known when the different strategies are simulated through the EIS model. It goes like this: *If we do X to address the high default rate on student loans, then the GRP will increase by Y. Or, if we do A to address the remedial training issue, then the GRP will increase by B.* This only reflects what the "what-if" analyses will show as we simulate the changes in the EIS model and trace the differences in the results.

THE EIS IS NOT A MARGINAL ANALYSIS

Simply put, the EIS is a total, not a marginal analysis of the kind typically conducted by economists for the purposes of recommending changes in how scarce resources are allocated among alternative and competing entities. Economics is largely about what happens at the margin—whether that last $100,000 dollars spent by the community college on a new parking lot will generate an increase in the GRP, or detract from it. We cannot tell this with the EIS—all we can do is to provide information on the total impact regardless of the performance of individual components.

When the impact metrics are strong and positive, the typical conclusion made is that the budget was spent wisely and the GRP increased as a result. That last $100,000 spent (or invested) is *presumed* to have yielded a positive return, although we do not know. It may well be that the spending in some areas generated losses (or the returns from that spending did not generate corresponding higher revenues), but spending in other areas generated gains that more than offset the losses. In the end, the results are positive as the gains more than cover the losses in the aggregate. Only economic theory through the efficacy of marginal analysis can sort this all out and provide clarity on the question of spending only up to the point where marginal revenues equal marginal costs (see below).

In the EIS, the college budget outlines the funding for the specific actions the college plans to undertake for the next year—let's call it a business plan A. In the minds of the college leaders, this plan reflects the agreements they reached to operate the college as efficiently as possible for one year. When an EIS is commissioned, we look at how well the college performed as measured by the economic impacts at the end of the analysis year. We do not compare and contrast different spending proposals B, C, or D that will have different regional impact outcomes. That's for the "what-if" analyses to sort out. What if we had spent our budget on proposal B (or C or D) instead of how we actually spent it? How would the EIS results have changed?

In economics we are always seeking to operate where profits are maximized, or (if you can remember the lessons from Econ 101 a few years back) where marginal revenues equal marginal costs. That is the sweet spot where spending the last dollar generates at least as much revenue as it adds to the cost. Our job as EIS analysts, however, is not to conduct a marginal economic analysis of the college's performance. We do not monitor whether the last dollar is well spent with at least a dollar's worth of revenue in return. Nor do we presume to ensure that the scarce resources available—the budget—are as optimally allocated as possible. The analysis is locked into the blueprint of business plan A.

We only *assume* that this plan reflects the best and most efficient spending choices available because the allocation of the budget was presumably subjected to appropriate due diligence and settled upon only after extensive internal political and budgetary negotiations. In the end, leaders settle on a spending plan they can live with, and that's the plan the EIS analyzes. Alternative courses of actions may have been considered up front, but rejected in favor of the one actually implemented. Everybody has 20/20 hindsight, however, and there are always questions of how the EIS results would have changed had we done things differently. With the EIS results, the model, and the databases in hand, it would be a relatively simple task to simulate the regional economic impact outcomes of those alternative budgets.

So, we only measure the impacts given the blueprint of business plan A. It probably is not a perfect plan, which means it does not reflect an economically optimal allocation of scarce resources. It may be poorly executed during the analysis year, or it may be constrained by counterproductive policies over which the colleges have no control. Every "notch" below an economically optimal allocation of resources is a "notch" to the detriment of the GRP (more on this topic in the next section).

The snapshot of college and regional data for one analysis year (budget, sources of revenues, student profiles, their educational achievements, and the regional data) describes the following:

- The college spends a budget of X.
- It serves Y students.
- The students achieve Z credits during the analysis year.
- Academic and vocational programs offered by the college are matched up with the regional economic base (industries, occupations, and demographics) to determine probable employment.

From this checklist, we calculate the economic impact the college has on the region it serves. Not factored into this analysis is whether budget X is too small or too large, whether Y students are too many or too few, whether Z credits accomplished on average per student is too low or just right, or whether the mix of programs offered is relevant to the region's economic base and is spot on or deficient.

Colleges sometimes conduct predictive analytics of student success because it allows the college leaders the luxury of favoring or disfavoring certain programs during the program budget negotiations. But once those budgetary decisions are made for this budget cycle, the college can still only accommodate X students given the size of the budget. Our job as EIS analysts is simply to generate the impact metrics as a reflection of how the colleges maneuvered given the current business environment.

As pointed out earlier, when the EIS measures are available, colleges typically call a press conference and announce the results, particularly if they are strong and positive. If this action is *all* the colleges do with the results, however, they are missing opportunities to greatly improve the ways many other issues are handled. To reiterate, the EIS results could easily serve as benchmark measures to test alternative courses of action—business plans B, C, and D intended to address other issues—*as if* they had been implemented at the beginning of the analysis year. The proof—moving the college closer to an optimal allocation of resources—would be the identification of the better business plan.

"WHAT-IF" ANALYSIS

Growing the GRP next year should be the Holy Grail for most state legislators, at least that is what most economists wishfully think. To that end—and to make the legislators look good—college leaders should target them with convincing and data-driven arguments to decide in favor of supporting the colleges. The EIS provides the means to do precisely this because it can be used to simulate credible estimates of changes in the GRP as different resource-allocation proposals are tested through "what-if" analyses. This is simply a way to measure what the EIS results *would have looked like* if different resource allocation decisions were made at the beginning of the analysis year.

With the EIS model and databases (college data and regional data) in hand, "what-if" analyses are a simple process of simulating changes and tracing how those changes will affect the results. What if we had enrolled 100 students in program A instead of the students *actually* enrolled in program B? How would that action have increased or decreased the GRP? The incremental changes would be introduced into the model and the results recalculated. If the change increases the GRP more than it adds to costs, it would have been a good move, otherwise not.

The secret sauce of this kind of analysis is linked to the communications skills of the college leaders. How well is the increase in GRP communicated to on-the-fence legislators to change their minds from a "no" to a "yes" vote? College leaders must be steeped in the EIS metrics, what they mean, how they were derived, and most importantly, what they mean for the regions their colleges serve. As any college president knows, changing the budgetary priorities and asking for more taxpayer money to implement them at any college is a major undertaking. It must be accompanied by elegant and well-articulated arguments rooted in attractive results based on hard and credible data. Securing a "yes" vote on requests for budgetary increases next year for a college (or colleges in the aggregate) always has a higher probability if the request is supported with hard data and analysis.[4] Examples of this kind of ("what-if") analysis would include:

- Tweaking the program mix offered to the students to better address issues like the high student default rate on loans (business plan B),
- Radically changing the program mix by eliminating some programs and adding others to address the same issues (business plan C), or
- Something different (business plan D).

College leaders should avoid the temptation to rely only on strong EIS results based on the current allocation of resources to justify new requests for more money from the state.[5] Business plans B, C, and/or D must be designed and simulated on the current EIS model to track how the current EIS results would change if these plans had been implemented at the beginning of the analysis year. Although the current EIS results are sufficiently convincing to some legislators, measuring results from an *improved allocation of resources* is far better than basing the requests for funding only on *what is*—the current allocation of resources. Getting closer to where we *ought* to be is the primary job of the college leadership once the EIS results are in hand. It is at that point where the results should be leveraged by inferring from the data where we could have been if resources had been allocated differently.

To add some economics flavor to this reasoning, any requests for funding increases made during legislative sessions should reflect a desire to move closer to the production possibilities frontier. The "what-if" analyses provide the measurements of the increases in GRP relative to the costs incurred to get there (for which the requests for increased funding are made). The chances for approval are enhanced, all else being equal, because the proposals are backed up by credible data, they reflect the taxpayers' interests, and they improve the allocation of scarce resources. All of this can be clearly communicated to the stakeholders as strong wins for both the colleges and the taxpayers.

A keen awareness of this one important lesson marks where the EIS leaves off and what comes next. *Building* on the EIS results through "what-if" analysis is the operative sentiment, not to rely too much on them alone for general advocacy in a legislative session intended to plan for the next year. The college leadership needs to use and leverage the EIS results as a part of their arguments, and to do so more effectively from *both* the taxpayers' and the college's perspectives.

A final note—of course, the results would change from a "what-if" analysis, but not always for the better. All we do here is simulate what we consider to be good ideas on how to move the needle for the college, how to improve on the current allocation of fixed resources. The scenarios we analyze have both costs and benefits, and, if the present value of the former is greater than the present value of the latter, then that particular scenario will not be in the portfolio for next year's budget request. Only the scenarios that show strong and feasible, positive results for the college will be survive the process and make it through as proposals.

DEALING WITH POLICIES

Communicating the next year's college agenda to legislators and other stakeholders is very much improved through "what-if" analyses using the EIS databases and results. That much should be abundantly clear by now. The arguments will be crisper, based on credible data and, therefore, not anecdotal, and they will cater to what *everyone* wants— the economic well-being of the region's population. This is truly a win-win argument, and certainly one the college leaders should become very adept at communicating to the stakeholders. Whether or not it will be enough to sway the legislators to vote in favor of the colleges is another question, but it *will* force them to think through what the economic consequences will be when they vote for or against the colleges, and that makes them more accountable for their decisions.

Before getting into the specifics of dealing with the policies that govern how community colleges behave in the marketplace, we first have some housekeeping to address—the separation of the things that can be controlled by the colleges and the things that cannot. Both can be at least partially resolved with the EIS results and databases.

Controlled by the Colleges

Once the budget for the college has been cast in stone for the year—all dollars are accounted for—its internal management is controlled by the college leaders. That money, everyone agrees, must now be spent as efficiently as possible. If not, there is room for improvement, and college leaders must beware of the itch they need to scratch to make that happen. At the beginning of the year, the budgetary decisions are locked in to pay for a specific program mix, building and maintaining the infrastructure, serving a student body of a certain size, local vendor purchases, and the salaries and benefits for faculty and staff. If an EIS has been commissioned for that year, the impacts of this spending, however efficient or inefficient it may be, will be measured at the end of the year.

Here's the rub. In the majority of cases the EIS results have been impressive, even though the college budgets may have been spent inefficiently. The results typically show that the colleges can claim credit for a significant portion of the regional GRP, sometimes more so than the impact that can be claimed by most other industries. So, is there really a need to rock the boat by questioning the efficiency with which things were done during the analysis year? The answer to that question is a resounding yes. The results could indeed be even better if the resources were allocated more efficiently. College leaders must develop a keen desire to avoid resting on their laurels just because the EIS results are strong. They should be in continuous search of ways to do better next year.

Doing better, however, is a challenge to say the least. No one has 20/20 hindsight, and the decisions made at the beginning of the year may turn out to have been altogether the wrong ones, or perhaps only slightly off key, when questioned later in the year. These discoveries are made as the year unfolds—they become lessons learned. Acting upon them, however, is a different story. Those who do are far ahead of the pack. These college leaders regard the discoveries as lessons learned, which they incorporate into the budget decisions for next year. Those who don't commit a grave mistake (and this happens too often). They assume that things are going well because the EIS results are strong, so no corrective action is needed.

A keen awareness of the possible mistake of doing X last year is the itch; testing the feasibility of doing Y next year is the scratch. This dynamic can emerge only when the EIS databases and results provide the platform for testing how resources could be allocated more efficiently next year. College leaders are much better equipped with credible data to analyze the feasibility of allocating more money to program A and less money to program B because of changing workforce needs in the region; or add entirely new programs and drop old ones for the same reasons. Having the ability to now conduct analyses with data they did not have before the EIS, they will be able to at least estimate how much the results could improve (or change) if resources were allocated differently.

If, for example, the most important issue for next year is to reduce the high default rate on student loans, a different mix of programs that would move more students into higher-paying jobs could be simulated and the changes to the GRP measured (more on this in chapter 6). The richness of the EIS data and results, supplemented by labor market data, will illuminate the pathways to much better decision making, and the EIS could become the catalyst that will help make the bolder decisions next year.

Program decisions are obviously hard because they are politically volatile. They involve internal politics, and any change in the status quo is never easy. They involve people and livelihoods, and perhaps the urgent problem of jealousies between programs. They impact morale. So, it is a balancing act, to be sure, and a college president must be skilled in making changes without ruffling too many feathers to continuously move the college toward the most efficient allocation of scarce resources possible.

This, in a nutshell, marks the importance of the college leadership to also assume a *taxpayer perspective* in how they advocate for the colleges. Decisions studiously avoided in the past because of the potential political fallout can now be made and justified by the EIS data and results. To always improve the internal allocation of resources will, in turn, improve the economic performance of the college, and that demonstrates taxpayer accountability—a sorely needed ingredient in the legislative process from the community college leadership. It should never be dulled by otherwise strong EIS results.

Not Controlled by the Colleges

Colleges also do not reach the goal of optimal allocation of resources because some policies, over which they have no control, constrain the ways they are managed. They are like unfunded mandates. Certainly not instituted with economic optimality in mind, these policies are accommodated by the colleges every day. As EIS analysts, we must take them as given and include them in the calculation of impacts. The results, although still strong and above threshold levels, only confirm what we already know anecdotally: that education pays. Strong results do not automatically mean that the college is run efficiently.

The existence of these policies is probably more detrimental to the regional economic well-being than if the college had been allowed to make its own decisions about its spending and tuition rates, for example. Varying in intensity between states, of course, the common features of the policies include state control over tuition rates, open-access policies and the resulting remedial training requirements, and state control over the program offering.

While put in place by well-meaning legislators to presumably reflect the best interests of the state's taxpayers, they often trigger a less-than-optimal allocation of scarce public (taxpayer) resources. The EIS results show the economic impacts with such policies in effect. We do not measure the extent to which their presence stunts the GRP. There is, however, ample economic reason to argue for their discontinuation, or at least to propose they be marginally changed, so that scarce taxpayer resources could be allocated more efficiently.

Arguing for changes to these policies, or outright discontinuation, however, is typically done based on anecdotal reasoning. College leaders lament the existence of these policies at conferences and in meetings, but the policies rarely change. Instead, the arguments can be a lot more effective if communicated with some punch and accompanied by some hard analysis, like using the EIS data in conjunction with "what-if" analyses to show by how much the EIS results will likely change if the college budgets were spent productively (as would be the case when the counterproductive policies are eliminated or changed).

Legislators need "ammunition" to support a different allocation of scarce taxpayer resources in the education sector. And that ammunition consists of credible data. Some policies are indeed counterproductive. Absent any changes, their continued presence will blunt the growth in GRP.

Step one is to clearly demonstrate that counterproductive policies are present and that colleges are obliged to accommodate them. Step two is to argue, with numbers, that changing the policies will substantially increase the GRP, including the reasons why. It becomes a matter of tracing the policy changes through the EIS model to derive the data-driven measurements of the extent to which they would impact the state's GRP. This approach should resonate more with the legislators and taxpayers than requesting funding only based on the college's desires and needs and not on how the change will affect the regional economy as a whole.

One counterproductive policy from the purely economic standpoint is the mandate for colleges in many states to maintain tuition rates at an artificially low level, which allows for open access for students who cannot otherwise afford or desire to attend four-year universities. Says Terry O'Banion about the Access Agenda: "The open-door philosophy encourages any student who has graduated from high school, obtained a GED, or is 18 years or older to enter college."[6]

The open-access policy *is* intended for benevolent purposes and, although it is generally perceived as a good community college policy, it also attracts the marginal students who otherwise would not attend college. And *that* is an economic negative. Community colleges essentially become the haven for not only the students who cannot afford the tuition, but also the ones least qualified and not at all ready for college, but still holding high-school diplomas.

The combined effect of low tuition and open access increases enrollment, often far over and beyond the capacity of the college infrastructure to accommodate it. Nearly half of the undergraduate students in the United States are enrolled in community colleges.[7] And far too many of them "arrive ill-prepared and, as a result, leave mired in debt without earning an income-boosting degree or career certification."[8] Community colleges have also built up their infrastructure over time to accommodate this influx of both the regular *and* ill-qualified students, and are obliged to ask for more money every year just to maintain it.

As with any enterprise, however, bigger is not always better, and colleges should never lose sight of the concept of optimality. From a taxpayer perspective, it is far better to serve an optimal number of students rather than the biggest possible student body calibrated to the artificial capacity set through policies. A state's capacity to serve students should ideally be adjusted to the demographic makeup of the state and/or region, the productivity of the regional workforce, and the workforce needs as expressed by the employers. It should not be calibrated to enrollment or tuition-rate policies established by state or regional government authorities. Policies such as tuition control and open access inadvertently put incentives and disincentives in place, and prospective students pick and choose the colleges partly because of the policies in place.

Discontinuing, or at least marginally changing, such policies will add considerably to the GRP of the regions served by the colleges—and that would be welcomed by the taxpayers. The size of the community-college student body in any state is, to a large extent, a reflection of the artificially low tuition and open-access policies. The rub, however, is that no college system would ever propose to adjust the funding level downward to accommodate only optimal-size student bodies. The chances for budgetary requests lower than previous years are practically zero. "Downward" is not in anyone's vocabulary; something else is needed, something different.

The reasons communicated for higher budgetary requests need to be different. Instead of couching funding increase requests in terms of what the college needs so that it can to do more of the same (using strong EIS results as sufficient justification), the requests should explicitly demonstrate how the *taxpayers would gain* as the college allocates scarce resources more efficiently. The objective of this new (or perhaps more correctly—nuanced) way of requesting more funds is to be aware of the other sectors competing for funding by deemphasizing the sole focus on the *college's needs*, but demonstrating a much broader perspective of how the *taxpayers* would gain from doing so.

An approach like this would be several moves ahead. The legislators' responsibility is to allocate scarce taxpayer money in such a way that gains in one sector must be greater than the expense of other sectors. It *is* a zero-sum game. The value of education, which the EIS measures, increases the colleges' *competitiveness* for funding. This is not only because the colleges can show the changes in the GRP in real numbers and the other sectors can't, they can also show that the (narrow) taxpayer ROI is also generally high. The increased tax collections from the higher earnings more than offsets the state tax appropriations and local property taxes needed to fund the college.

Recall from chapter 3, this means in essence that the colleges subsidize the other sectors serving the state. Were it not for the existence of the colleges, state income taxes and/or property taxes would have to increase for the state to maintain the current level of services provided for *all* sectors in the state.

The focus, therefore, should not only be on increasing the impacts measured with the EIS as a result of bigger budgets next year. Instead, it should be on leveraging the EIS results by pointing to how the colleges could be more accountable to the taxpayers. Presidents and governing boards should use their intimate knowledge of the political issues, GRP, the economic base, the demographic makeup of the region, and the status and productivity of the regional workforce to sway legislators to change counterproductive policies for the better. The EIS results become the vehicle to substantially enrich the arguments with data-driven measures instead of anecdotes. And, not to forget, when the GRP is increased and taxpayers are better off because of the colleges, the other sectors funded by the state benefit as well.

A Thought Experiment

Suppose the rumor mill has it that the state support for colleges is slated for a 5 percent cut—enough of a cut to make some college presidents lose their sleep, particularly if the size of the student body is expected to increase. If recent EIS results are not available, they begin the process of internally preparing their colleges to tighten their belts. The usual approach includes consideration of the following: substituting adjunct faculty for tenured faculty to save costs, increasing class size and compromising the quality of the education supplied, or making the difficult decisions to cut some programs. They do all of this in anticipation of the 5 percent cut in the budget.

But if recent EIS results are available, an entirely different strategy could be devised. Suppose the 5 percent cut in state support is to be implemented across the board for all the sectors, not just the community colleges. That's the reality. When drilling down, however, there is plenty of room for negotiations *between the sectors* while still maintaining the overall cut of 5 percent.

Strong EIS results for the colleges mean they have a leg up, and an opportunity. The first case to be made is that the colleges generate more tax revenues for the state than they take out in the form of tax appropriations. At a first glance, therefore, this suggests that a 5 percent cut is economic folly if applied to the colleges, all else being equal.

The reality, however, is that cutting all sectors in budgetary tight years is a fact of life, and so the legislators' hands are tied. They must represent the taxpayers as they decide who gets how much (or how much less) in a zero-sum game. Typically, who wins the most is the sector with the most political clout. And, in the education sector, the K–12 system and public universities generally have more political clout than community colleges unless the community colleges have the impact results to prove otherwise.

The political interplay between sectors, however, offers an opportunity to advocate for the community colleges more effectively with the EIS results than without them. A second, more granular, argument to be made is this: a 5 percent cut will have measurable economic consequences because it would translate into *numbers of students not served*. From there it is an easy task to run the analysis to determine the economic impact those students *would have* generated if the cuts were not made.[9]

To illustrate, a college system must first derive a credible measure of how many fewer students would attend the college if the 5 percent cut were implemented. Suppose, hypothetically, the current state funding for the colleges amounts to a total of $1 billion, the enrollment is 175,000 students, or the state support amounts to $5,714 per student. A 5 percent cut amounts reduces the budget to $950 million, or the state can now only accommodate a total of 166,250 students with the same level of support. This amounts to a drop in the student headcount of

8,750 students, based on the ratio of taxpayer funding to students served.

The focus now shifts to the 8,750 fewer students who would not attend because the colleges insist on maintaining the current support level per student. These (8,750 fewer) students will subsequently not enter the workforce with higher earnings, nor will they pay more in taxes. Indeed, statistics show that these students, deprived of their education, are more likely to commit crimes, become incarcerated, receive unemployment or welfare support, and continue with poorer health habits. These are all measurable economic consequences so long as the EIS databases are available.

On the positive side, the taxpayers would save $50 million with this budget cut. But on the negative side, if the cumulative present value of the tax collections that would have been realized from the higher earnings of the 8,750 (fewer) students exceeds the $50 million saved initially, then the taxpayers would be far better off with not cutting the budget for community colleges and saving the taxpayers some money initially. In addition, the taxpayers would not benefit from the cumulative value of the social benefits that would have been realized if the budget were not cut.

In the end, mounting data-driven arguments with a measurable economic impact consequence should gain the attention of the legislators, especially when the arguments are made collectively on behalf of all the community colleges in the state. Perhaps it would result in a shallower cut, say 2 percent, for the colleges instead of the slated 5 percent cut. Two percent is far less than 5 percent and could add up to a significant amount of money restored to the colleges.

The sticking point, however, is that a shallower cut for the colleges would have to be at the expense of a steeper cut elsewhere (see discussion of community colleges vs. the K–12 system below). If a college is facing a budget shortfall, a president should fight long and hard to minimize the shortfall to get a relatively bigger share of a shrinking pie. If a 5 percent cut is offered (and a cut in some years is a certainty), holding it to a 2 percent cut for the community colleges would be far better. It is a one-way street—more is better during years of plenty, or the avoidance of steep cuts in favor of shallower cuts during lean years. Using the EIS metrics, college administrators could effectively lobby for funding.

Community college presidents need to be adept at convincing legislators that investing in community colleges increases the GRP more so than investing in the universities, or in K–12. Or, a broader argument is that investing in education in general increases the GRP more so than investing in health or welfare. The bottom line: the economic arguments for the colleges should not be made in isolation from the requests made by other competitors for public funding.

All of this said, it should be clear that college presidents need to display a familiarity about the economics behind the EIS results that overshadows the understanding of their peers. If resources (factors of production) are misallocated (which they, in all probability, are) then simply requesting more money to do more of the same is not effective, at least not in the long run. Context counts. College presidents who use economic information to argue for increased budgets, however, should do so being informed by not only the EIS results and what they mean, but also by the economic attractiveness of the other sectors competing for funding. It is not as simple as merely arguing that more money begets better impact results.

The EIS results themselves may all be great, but this alone does not necessarily provide the most compelling case for staying the course while doing little different. Positive results do not give sufficient reason to pat oneself on the back for a job well done—they are part of the reason, but certainly not all of it.

THE EIS IS NOT AN ADVOCACY STUDY

Is it the responsibility of the college presidents to advocate for the college with the EIS results? Yes, absolutely, but only when the results are strong enough and only *after the study has been completed.* If so, they should be broadcast to stakeholders in the regional communities, and the college leaders can accept the applause and use the positive PR as a recruiting tool for students and faculty.

But it is not the purpose of the EIS *analysts* to be advocates for a college, at least not at the outset. The results are unknown when we begin the study, and they are what they are when we finish it. If the data from the colleges combined with the data from the regions do not generate positive results, then our obligation is to objectively report the results we calculate. The EIS provides an economic audit of a college's operations in much the same way Deloitte, or another third party, would conduct an audit of a business's financial statements. As such, the study itself is not an instrument intended to be used for advocacy purposes at the outset. That occurs *after the fact*, after the results are shown to be strong and outperform alternative uses of public funds.

Of the utmost importance, therefore, is that college presidents fully understand what the results reflect and what they don't. Only then can they legitimately compare between alternative uses of public funds and make their case for a larger share of the funding dollars. Will an additional dollar spent on the community college outperform (higher ROI) an additional dollar spent on the health sector, or the transportation sector? Only the net numbers will allow for such comparisons.

An example of an advocacy study would be to knowingly use the same basic methodological approach but only present the gross numbers (higher must be better or more impressive) and not inform the reader about the difference. The burden of failing to discern the difference falls on the president and the governing board—they need to be sufficiently literate in the EIS mechanics to understand the risks.

For many colleges, however, advocacy is key, and it shows up in how they conduct the studies. This is typical when the college's internal economics departments become the analysts. In an ideal world, the EIS approach should be fairly standard, and the metrics are what they are. Sometimes they are excellent and afford the opportunity to advocate, but if sometimes they are less than stellar, as the saying goes—silence is golden. There are times when the results are tepid at best, and advocating for the college on their basis would not be advisable.

CONCLUSION

To conclude, this chapter is about what an EIS is not. Whereas an EIS provides critical information on the extent to which the college impacts the regional economic well-being, it does *not* recommend how the college can do better and how the economic impacts can be increased. The EIS describes what is—that's as far as it goes. Now it is incumbent on the college leaders to take the next steps by using these results to plan for next year.

In this sense, it has limits, and those limits are defined in terms of economic theory. The EIS is not a marginal analysis, which is how economic theory is used to determine maximum profitability of an institution's operation, whether it is selling a product or providing a service. Nor does it provide guidance on how to *optimally* allocate scarce resources—through the production possibilities frontier—relative to how community colleges *actually* allocate those resources. There are many ways community colleges *could* allocate resources that would add more economic impact to the region. The EIS, however, measures the economic impacts based on observed behavior, not on optimal behavior.

The chapter also describes the potential usefulness of the EIS as a springboard for how to compete well for a bigger share of an increasingly scarce resource from the state taxpayers. State funding is still the lifeblood of community colleges, and it is worthwhile to compete well for their share of the fixed resources available. College leaders, therefore, need to go beyond the EIS results and always be on the lookout for better and more efficient ways, plus have the numbers available that prove their case. To that end, it is far better to come to the table well prepared and advocate armed with strong EIS results, but to do so from a taxpayer perspective instead of advocating from the college's perspective only.

NOTES

1. An Emsi economist colleague, Tim Nadreau, was responsible for developing the production possibilities theoretical construct in the context of community colleges. Through his work, it became abundantly clear that strong EIS results do not necessarily equate to a "job well done." The fact that most (if not all) community colleges operate well below the production possibilities frontier, yet still generate strong EIS results, should tell college presidents never to cease looking for ways to improve. Never be satisfied with just strong EIS results.

2. The Aspen Institute, *College Excellence Program: Selection Process*, 2019, http://highered.aspeninstitute.org/aspen-prize-program/selection-process/.

3. This should not be confused with continuity of the approach. Analysts conducting an EIS should use the same general approach for studies separated by two or more years. This provides continuity. However, advances in theory

and modeling functional relationships between variables may have changed incrementally during that time period, which makes the comparison of the results between the studies difficult at best.

4. At Emsi we have been building labor market information software for over a decade to connect the specific labor market needs in any region to the programs offered at the higher-education institutions. Our data is as recent and as granular as possible. With this data we can measure where and how wide and deep the occupation and education gaps are for any industry or region in the country. This information allows college program planners to effectively calibrate their programs to meet the regional needs. If the college already subscribes to Emsi's Analyst software, all the building blocks for what-if analysis are in place. Emsi's Analyst is software that contains all the economic and workforce data needed in one place: industries, occupations and earnings, input/output functionality, job postings, skills, college programs, and demographics. Its wealth of data and welcoming interface make objective analysis of any proposed development scenario easy.

5. Actually, we all do this—the temptation is sometimes very strong. Great results *should* mean a job well done, and they provide bragging rights. But our strong argument here is to change the mindset of the college leaders from one of a "job well done and go do likewise next year" as evidenced by the great EIS results, to one that reflects "we're still eager to improve." This means that measuring the "what-if" scenario is only the beginning, and the planning for next year should be full of changes that seek to improve on the allocation of resources.

6. Terry O'Banion, *Access, Success, and Completion: A Primer for Community College Faculty, Administrators, Staff, and Trustees* (Chandler, AZ: League for Innovation in the Community College, 2013).

7. Janell Ross, "Is Open-Access Community College a Bad Idea?" *The Atlantic*, June 23, 2014.

8. Ibid.

9. "Students not served" should, of course, not be confused with the (assumed) oversupply of students served under the mandate of the (in our opinion, counterproductive) open-access policy and the fact that community colleges are obliged to serve remedial students. The term "not served" refers to qualified students who cannot be accommodated because of budgetary restrictions.

5

MOVING THE NEEDLE

Economics and Politics

ECONOMICS

As the perception goes, economists don't agree on much. Prices go up, and half of us call it good and the other half call it bad. The Federal Reserve Bank is tightening the interest rate and we are for and against. Education costs are increasing, and we weigh in with conflicting arguments on why or why not to raise or lower tuition rates. What we vociferously argue for or against is probably more aligned with where we find ourselves on the political spectrum than is the case with most other technical professions. Our discipline lends itself to right and left–type debates, whereas the physics discipline doesn't get into that. Atoms don't care about political leanings, but interest rates do.

Common to all economists, however, is that we agree on the fundamentals of economic theory just as much as other disciplines agree on their theoretical backbone. We agree on the role of prices as an allocating mechanism, the laws of supply and demand, and that there is such a concept as an optimal allocation of scarce resources. And when the results of an economic impact study (EIS) show strong and positive impacts on the economy, we rejoice. To be sure, we have experienced much rejoicing over the majority of impact studies we have completed for colleges over the past 19 years. Education pays, and now we have the evidence to prove it.

The economic measures of an EIS, as error-free as possible, should not be controversial or politically laden, even though they are often attacked vociferously by opponents to increased funding requests based on those results. For this reason, college leaders must take the trouble to discern illegitimate from legitimate criticisms and familiarize themselves with the analytical process. They need to understand the meaning of the results, and most importantly, to know that the analysts commissioned to carry out the study were actually measuring net economic impacts, not contributions. When doing so, they will be able to defend the measures generated with confidence. Those who ignore this, however, risk making illegitimate political points if they are recipients of EIS measures that are *presented* as impacts but, in fact, are not.

POLITICS

We have said it before, and now say it again—politics trumps economics. We can carefully lay out the economic rationale for doing something, or not doing it, and it means little if we are not also conscious of the political realities surrounding any issue. It is for political reasons that we generally don't tell the *other side of the story*—the one we ignore or conveniently forget. The other side of the story consists of the unseen effects as in the *broken window principle* discussed in chapter 1. Another one that college presidents should always consider is the reality of competing demands for the fixed amount of public dollars available each year. This means that the presidents must learn to walk in the legislators' shoes for a moment to consider what *their* mandate is, which is to look out for the taxpayers. This is where the politics of it all becomes real.

The main reason why impact studies are conducted is, indeed, to provide the college president with the best possible arguments to win budgetary battles. This includes making it a lot easier for the legislators to support the colleges. Virtually all of the issues that colleges grapple with can easily be boiled down to—or solved by—dollars and cents. The EIS is an important tool in this process. Strong results are conveniently powerful in making arguments for the college, but they only go a part of the distance. College presidents and governing boards should know that the budgetary battles cannot be easily won only on the strength of these results because of the *competing demands for the available public dollars* (K–12 education, universities, health, transportation, public assistance, correction centers, and a sprinkling of others).

Just as a household must balance the returns of education, food, clothing, housing, and healthcare, so the legislature and governor must balance the high returns of education with the other demands of the state. Budgets are finite, and while impacts and investments may be feasible and even profitable, this doesn't mean we get to neglect the other initiatives in the state. Presidents can and should be leaders in this area by using some of their funds to support the research and larger mission of their municipal and state bodies.

These competing demands from *all* sectors comprise the main preoccupation of the legislators. They cannot address the colleges' needs and aspirations in isolation from other sectors; needs and aspirations must be dealt with in the context of the funding demands for all the sectors. It behooves college presidents and government boards, therefore, to be acutely aware of this dynamic and craft their messaging with that context in mind. In short, they need to account for the other half of the story—the legislators' mandates as stewards of the public's money.

Given the competing demands for funding, legislators should be courted with this in mind. It is not only about the needs and aspirations of the college, it is also about what the other sectors are requesting too. The Center on Budget and Policy Priorities shows how state taxes are spent on average for the United States (table 5.1).[1]

These are the straight averages. The percentages obviously differ between states, but in each state, the legislators' job is to decide on how much each sector will receive from the state's resources. The sum of the

Table 5.1. State Spending Categories

K–12 education	25%
Higher education (universities and community colleges)	13%
Medicaid and children's health insurance programs	17%
Transportation	5%
Public assistance	1%
Corrections	5%
All other (employees' pensions, local governments, etc.)	34%
Total	100%

education categories receives the most funds compared to the other individual categories (25% + 13% = 38%). The community colleges are funded by the 13 percent spent on higher education. Of that amount, however, 60 percent is used to fund universities, and only a lopsided 40 percent is spent on community college education, divided among the roughly 1,200 publicly supported community colleges in the United States.[2]

This is where the budgetary battle lines are drawn.

Technically, community colleges compete for funding with all sectors receiving state funding. In reality, however, the more intense competition is between the actors tapping into the education funds. The competition between education and the other sectors is typically low, but between K–12, community colleges, and universities, the competition is fierce. When universities see that some community college programs are successful and profitable, they often create their own similar programs and then greatly dilute the profitability. Community colleges need to make the case to the legislature that funding per student is higher at universities, and that when the universities engage in this "scope creep," it is costing the taxpayers more without return.

More often than not, however, the community colleges lose the battle and only receive what's left over, being squeezed in between K–12 and the public universities. Of course, community colleges are sometimes politically in vogue and receive more funding at the expense of the K–12 and university sectors, but those budget years are relatively rare.

State appropriations for community colleges have trended downward over the past 20 years, particularly when we include local government (property tax) funding.[3] The battleground for higher-education dollars is largely between community colleges and public universities. Both obviously merit public funding because they provide valuable economic services to citizens in general.

The question is how to divide the scarce state taxpayer dollars between the two sectors to ensure that the money will be optimally spent. From both perspectives, increasing the funding of one must be at the expense of decreasing funding for the other. If the current distribution of funding between the two sectors is not optimal now, state taxpayers, through their legislative representatives, should change the distribution for good economic reasons. And good economic reasons are best portrayed by the returns taxpayers will experience from investing in either sector.

It is, therefore, the responsibility of the leadership for both the community colleges and universities to come to the table as well prepared as possible with EIS results based on recent data. Also included should be the proposals for changes in the funding structure between the sectors backed up with data-driven analysis of the extent to which they will increase the regional GRP if implemented. This discussion is the *purpose* of legislative sessions.

The first challenge for the legislators is to assess which institutions benefit the region or state the most—the community colleges or the universities?[4] This obviously is a challenging task, and not one we are seeking to resolve here. We are certainly in favor of *both* sectors, because education is generating returns to both students and taxpayers that far exceed threshold levels. And when these sectors generate those kinds of returns, by definition, society at large is better off with than without them.

The differences between the EIS results for community colleges and universities, however, are significant in their interpretation, although the metrics are the same. The university regions are larger, and in some cases extend far beyond state boundaries. Their funding focus, therefore, must be more expansive, including perhaps a greater reliance on federal dollars (higher percentages) instead of state taxpayer dollars. Universities can be considered more like destination schools that draw students from outside the state far more so than the community colleges, and so perhaps they should rely relatively more on federal funding sources.

Community college students, on the other hand, have a greater propensity to remain in their home regions after exiting, and thereby add more productivity value for their regions, than do university students. The latter tend to be more mobile, even to the point of taking jobs in faraway states, as shown in table 5.2.[5] Based on the sample of 364 colleges and 135 universities, approximately 90 percent of the community college students settled in the region served by the colleges after completing their studies compared to an average of 73 percent for universities.

Another argument community college leaders can invoke for more funding relative to the universities is that the rewards to education for

Table 5.2. Students Settling In-Region

Year	Sample	Sample	Remaining-In-State (%)
2012	Colleges	49	90
	Universities	1	73
2013	Colleges	110	94
	Universities	93	69
2014	Colleges	59	79
	Universities	9	78
2015	Colleges	32	93
	Universities	10	63
2016	Colleges	76	92
	Universities	10	73
2017	Colleges	38	94
	Universities	12	75
Average	**Colleges**	**364**	**90**
	Universities	**135**	**73**

Source: Emsi EIS Database

the majority of their students tend to be greater than for university students for the time and money spent. Students who attend college from one year shy of a high-school diploma to high school plus two years (including the associate degree) happen to receive the biggest bump in earnings for their efforts. The earnings function tends to be steeper for this time period and educational effort, on average—steeper than between the associate-degree level (two years post high school) to four years (to and including a bachelor's degree); see table 5.3.[6]

Of course, this does not mean that community college students earn more; in fact, they generally don't. What it does mean is that the benefit/cost ratio is consistently higher for students who attend community college relative to all subsequent education levels. The rewards to education increase at an increasing rate with education up to and including the associate degree, and then continue to increase but at a decreasing rate for the higher-education levels.

A third argument is that more community college students are also gainfully employed (at least part-time) while attending college (68 percent) than university students (57 percent), so they invest less.[7] Their opportunity cost of time, therefore, is lower than it is for university

Table 5.3. ROI, Community Colleges and Universities

Metrics	Colleges	Universities
Rate of return	12%	8%
Benefit/cost ratio	3.0	2.2

Source: Emsi EIS Database

students. This is another reason that the return on investment (ROI) for community college students is generally higher.

In the battle for public funds, community college leaders should use the relatively low tuition argument at their institutions in the zero-sum game of competing for total student enrollment in the higher-education sector. Because tuition rates are significantly lower at the community colleges, it is far less expensive for students to enroll there for the first two years of their college career and then transfer than it is to attend the full four years at a public university. To this, we can add the incentive that community colleges enroll the lion's share of Pell-eligible students in higher education. For many of these students, attendance costs them literally nothing, or close to zero. The student ROI, therefore, is higher because the costs are significantly lower.

"FREE" COMMUNITY COLLEGES

One (perhaps unfortunate) consequence of consistently strong EIS results is that legislators and politicians tend to draft policies on the backs of results like these without thinking them all the way through. If education pays off as well as we have documented over the past two decades, why not do more of the same and continue to fund the colleges with abandon? One such policy development is reflected in the momentum to make community colleges "free." This policy is now a reality in 11 states and several more (at least nine) are expected to jump on the bandwagon.[8] The more money made available by the taxpayers and other funding sources, the more economic benefits the colleges can heap upon the regions served. It's a win-win situation. As well put by Bob Luebke of the Covitas Institute:[9]

- Calling something free doesn't make it free. Nothing in life is free. It's simply a matter of who pays the costs.
- If a college education has value, why give it away?
- If college becomes free for students, colleges will attract more young people who are not suited for college and more students will major in fields with little or no market value.

Nevertheless, making the community colleges "free" is the conclusion drawn by many, including many college presidents and some economists as well, using the EIS results as supporting (and sometimes convincing) arguments. Why not go all the way and make them "free" and therefore boost enrollment so that the economic impacts can increase even further? Remove the budgetary shackles, and the economy will thrive even more. This is essentially what the Obama administration proposed, using EIS results in support of their arguments.

The proposal was met with enthusiasm and dread from both ends of the political spectrum. To set the stage, it is quite obvious that community colleges are significant economic engines, as we have demonstrated since 2000, and in our (2014) nationwide economic impact study conducted for the American Association of Community Colleges (AACC).[10] A majority of prominent economists have also reasoned from different perspectives that the public benefits from education exceed the public (taxpayer) costs of providing it (see chapter 3). Students attend college, become more productive and receive higher earnings as a result, and therefore pay more in taxes, and this is in addition to the state government savings, which are quite significant as well. It is a benevolent and measurable circle. One could easily make the argument, therefore, that the more we spend on community colleges, the better off we are from an economic well-being perspective.

Given all of this, is there a downside to taxpayers being asked to invest more? The proposal by the Obama administration was to save a full-time community college student $3,800 in tuition per year on average to benefit roughly nine million students each year.[11] This means that taxpayers would pay an additional $34.2 billion per year in tuition support, tantamount to an increase of 43 percent over current funding levels. Following are a few points to consider from an economics perspective about such a proposal.

Optimum Level of Spending

As discussed earlier, the EIS generates results based on a snapshot of one year's worth of operations by blending regional and college data. Because it is a "total"—not a "marginal"—analysis, the snapshot captures the average impact based on the current combination of funding, faculty and staff numbers, and student achievements. What college leaders need to know about this snapshot is that there are diminishing returns to educational spending—more is not always better.

If the results are strong, based on a specific level of spending, it does not follow that more spending will continue to yield more benefits in a linear fashion. At some point, diminishing returns to additional spending will emerge. Whether we have already reached that point is the question. If we have *not yet* reached the optimal level of funding, more targeted spending to reach it is better. If we have *already reached* or passed the optimal level, however, any additional spending on the colleges will generate a gross regional product (GRP) lower than it would be if the money had been optimally allocated.

The latter case simply means that too much money has been withdrawn from the taxpayers to have a slowing-down effect on the GRP. Although the EIS results are generally attractive, we make no inference on whether the institution has reached the optimal level of spending or not, or gone beyond it. In the vast majority of cases we have only shown that, for the investment component, the results *are* attractive in that they meet or exceed threshold levels. In other words, they outperform alternative investments given comparable levels of risk. What we don't know is how attractive they could have been had resources been optimally allocated. On the regional impact side, the GRP does indeed increase because of the college, but whether that increase is as high as it could be is another question.

These results only demonstrate what we know intuitively, that college education *generally* pays, which gives college presidents presumed bragging rights to their boards, legislators, and constituents. For some colleges, the average returns are *not* favorable to the taxpayers, which means that curtailment, elimination, or restructuring is implied by the study results. For the majority of colleges, however, the results do not enhance the argument that more spending would generate still better results.

Spending Additional Money: The Impacts

If a marginal analysis of the "free" tuition proposal were conducted, it would focus on *new* costs and benefits as a result of increasing the amount of money the colleges have to spend.

But here's the problem.

While free tuition will allow many students to enroll who were previously unable to due to financial reasons, it will also beckon students who were previously not motivated to enroll due to lack of academic ability. The EIS results reported would then reflect numbers of students enrolled under *current* conditions, including remedial students plus those who enroll because of artificially low tuition rates and open-access policies. Many of these students would *not* have enrolled unless the existing policy environment and subsidies made it easy for them to do so. Moreover, adding fuel to the fire, this would have the effect of stressing the existing college infrastructure to its limits, and beyond, and thus triggering an increase in demand for yet more funding to accommodate this growth in the number of students.

Too many academically unsuitable students also translates directly into the problems we frequently observe today—that students cannot find jobs because they are ill prepared for the workforce. Although the Obama administration proposal mandates that in order for students to receive free tuition, they "must maintain a 2.5 GPA and make steady progress toward completing their program," and that the colleges must "offer programs that are either (1) academic programs that fully transfer credits to local public four-year colleges and universities, or (2) occupational training programs with high graduation rates and lead to in-demand degrees and certificates,"[12] it may also lead to the enrollment of more students who are far less motivated to pursue the kind of education that leads to well-paying careers, and so they cannot find jobs other than low-paying ones. What has really been gained:

- for the GRP if these additional students cannot find jobs when exiting the college?
- for the students if the student ROI falls below threshold levels?
- for the taxpayers if the taxpayer ROI falls below threshold levels, because these additional students are less likely to add any productivity to the regional workforce?[13]

- for the employers if the signal of added productivity attributable to the employees' education becomes meaningless? If everyone has the associate degree it is no longer scarce, so it loses value in the marketplace.[14]

For these reasons we would not expect the strong results from the EIS to continue to hold. For some people, anything "free" lacks the motivating ingredient that translates into a greater willingness to learn and eventually apply the skills learned in the workforce.

ISSUES THAT MATTER

We have established earlier what an EIS is (chapter 2), or is not (chapter 3), and how the results can help college presidents address other technical or political issues. In chapters 6 and 7 we shall get a little more specific about what some of these issues are and how colleges with the EIS results can, at least partly, shed some light on these issues and be useful in their resolution.

What we know so far from the EIS is that the larger the regional impact and the higher the student and taxpayer ROIs, the better the college's performance is perceived. As soon as those numbers are published and "digested" by the stakeholders, however, they become history, and the battle for next year's funding begins. What can the college do differently next year to incorporate the lessons learned, at least partially, to resolve political and managerial issues and improve on that performance?

Improving on last year's performance is no easy task, however, as college leaders well know. It takes ingenuity to chart a different direction for the college next year while not looking like last year's performance was suboptimal or faulty. Besides, since the funding battles take place mostly in the public square, college presidents must be prepared to defend their proposals for action for next year's direction with both economic and political arguments while not atoning for any lingering perception that last year's performance may have been less than optimal.

As discussed at length earlier, no longer does it suffice to justify why more money is needed next year with arguments based on strong EIS results only. These results do carry the water on how well the colleges did for the students and the regional taxpayers last year, *but not relative to the benefits other public investments might have generated*. State and federal resources are tightening, and there is little evidence of any impending reversal of this trend. Legislators and decision makers rightfully require additional scrutiny and stronger justification of the funding requests by the community colleges. Quite simply, the colleges need to grow in their sophistication in how they fight for their share of the funding.

One recommendation is to use "what-if" analyses as discussed in chapter 4, which requires the availability of the EIS results. Growing in sophistication means that the results should be *leveraged* even more. This, of course, means that the colleges may have to contract for additional services to prepare the proposals to present to the legislators. At least, these three points should be included in the scope-of-work:

- why the actions are proposed (e.g., the specific issues addressed)?
- what are the measurable costs?
- what are the measurable benefits?

If the present value of the benefits exceeds the present value of the costs, then the GRP will increase as a result of the actions taken. It is a miniature economic feasibility study of proposed activities. It is also a simple step of walking in the shoes of the legislators, speaking their language, and (let's be honest) making them look good when they decide in favor of the colleges' requests. Having credible and actual economic impact estimates available as proof of looking out for the taxpayers is a political home run if communicated well to the right audiences. It is a far different approach than using the EIS results to advocate for the colleges only.

"Moving the needle" is the same as improving the allocation of scarce resources. The quest to progress toward optimality should be ever-present. In the previous chapter, we discussed this process in the context of a theoretical construct of a production possibilities frontier. We ideally want to operate *on* the frontier where the colleges (theoretically) no longer can allocate resources any more efficiently. Colleges should always be conscious of, and strive to do, precisely this by keeping a watchful eye on improvement opportunities previously considered to be too difficult to "sell" in a politically charged environment. Most (if not all) colleges operate well below the frontier, however, because of inefficiencies in the internal allocation of resources, and also the presence of counterproductive higher-education policies that siphon off scarce resources from the core mission of the colleges.

Moving the needle is defined by implementing actions that increase the GRP. Targeted analyses drawing on the EIS databases to simulate the extent to which an action would trigger a change in the results is the simplest way. An example of an action would be to replace old Program A with 150 students with new Program B with a capacity to enroll 150 students as well, and determine whether this would have a significant and positive impact on the EIS results. The difference in the GRP is determined by simply measuring how much more the students from Program B are likely to earn on average relative to the students from Program A and trace that change through with the EIS model, all else being equal.

Of course, there are nuances to this kind of analysis, such as the degree of added difficulty in completing Program B as opposed to Program A. But such nuances could easily be simulated with credible assumptions in submodeling routines whereby the dropout rate for Program B would be slightly higher than average than for Program A.[15] Taking all of these nuances into account, the final numbers are derived and then plugged into the EIS model. The calculated differences in the overall EIS results (including the ROI results for the students and taxpayers), would then be generated, while all else in the EIS model would remain unchanged.

The analysts carrying out these "what-if" analyses should prepare short reports with narrative on the context for the proposed change, and whether the benefits exceed or fall short of the costs. If benefits exceed costs, it is like a rising tide lifting all boats—it defines progress. And economic progress for all taxpayers is the alpha and omega. All issues, whatever they are, acted upon aggressively (or tepidly), invariably contribute to or detract from the GRP.

On the investment side, things are a bit more complicated.

Acting upon the issues will affect both the student and taxpayer ROIs, but not necessarily in the same direction as the GRP. They are independent analyses. The GRP may increase as a result of the change, but the ROIs may decrease. For example, a change in the program mix may lead to more students eligible for higher paying jobs. True, but it is also a fact that the new program mix may be costlier. If the cost of completing the course is double, then the question is whether the earning benefit outweighs the additional costs. If not, the ROI will be lower. Avoiding these issues to steer clear of the certain political battles will always be a losing strategy in the long run.

College presidents go to work every day feeling the political, administrative, economic, and managerial burdens of running a public, taxpayer-funded institution. In so doing, they are pressured from all directions to "do something" about the issues of the day. Some of the more persistent national and regional issues include the following:

- the high default rates on student loans;
- the imbalance between the supply and demand for skills in the workforce;
- low graduation or completion rates;
- tuition and how it affects enrollment;
- the remedial problem; and
- annexing tax districts

This checklist of issues is discussed in chapters 6 and 7. They are worrisome, and college leaders must artfully deal with them so as to minimize the displeasure of both sides of the political spectrum.

The EIS results and databases are useful in putting all of these issues at least partially to bed by measuring the extent to which the GRP would increase from the activities proposed to address them. The results and databases make it a lot easier to be bold in proposing new activities, because the political fallout will be blunted. If the proposals are well analyzed and backed up by credible data rather than by anecdotes only, opponents will see their arguments become significantly weaker and carry less weight in the public square. Moreover, the proposals should also resonate with the legislators and decision makers who will benefit from the accolades sure to follow for having facilitated the increases in the GRP.

In the following two chapters, we seek to provide some depth and clarity about the EIS results and how college leaders can use them to build credible arguments in support of their vision for the future, to defuse political opposition, and to do so with minimal friction among the stakeholders. Being bold and aggressive in this kind of political environment where even small changes can trigger a flood of negativity cannot be done in a vacuum—it requires lots of data and analyses to leave no stone unturned. There must be good reasons for even considering these actions. And, those reasons must be data-driven, not just anecdotal.

CONCLUSION

A college president can, at least for some time, avoid entering the political fray that any and all economic development issues bring to local communities. But not for very long. The community college is right in the middle of it, because the college provides the main ingredient—a well-qualified workforce. Every regional stakeholder wants economic development, but only in certain forms. Most want high-tech businesses, for example, but probably less so manufacturing (affecting the environment), or retail (low paying, probably). Hence the political fray.

Or, a college president can be front and center and enter the politics of it all with boldness and exhibiting leadership in the process. This means making some unpopular decisions, such as cutting programs and replacing them with new ones from time to time, or not caving to all the union demands, or perhaps favoring regional demands for skills at the expense of local demands. Economic development leadership is all about moving the needle in measurable ways with all stakeholders on board and rowing in the same direction.

Not everyone in the community will be equally pleased, but then again—pleasing everyone at all times is an impossibility. Always taking actions to increase the GRP, while ensuring the investments made by the students and taxpayers are attractive, are both political and economic winners. Everyone benefits from strong economic development. A community college, therefore, should chart courses of action that benefit all, not just the college or a few of the regional employers. In economic theory we call this the process of identifying Pareto-optimal moves, that is, "changes in policy that make some people better off without making anyone else worse off."[16]

Perhaps the biggest political issue of the day is that of "free" community colleges. The word "free" is put in quotation marks because it is free to students, but not to taxpayers. If college leaders are to walk in the shoes of the legislators, as we recommend here, then they should carefully consider the economic ramifications of this movement.

Yet, many have and the momentum is alive and well. Several states are considering legislation that will make this happen, in addition to the 11 states that have already adopted such a policy. It is our opinion that society will, in the long run, get a lot more students attending college who would be better off pursuing endeavors other than a college education. College is not for everyone. We believe that an influx of such students will exert a negative pressure on the investment returns to education and eventually to the point where they will dip below threshold levels. The GRP growth will eventually stagnate as well for two reasons: (a) because the regional employers will not hire ill-prepared students, and (b) the taxpayers will have paid for all this "free" tuition with money that would have grown the economy more if it had been used to fund other sectors.[17]

NOTES

1. The Center on Budget and Policy Priorities, "Policy Basics: Where Do Our Tax Dollars Go?" cbpp.org, April 24, 2017, https://www.cbpp.org/research/state-budget-and-tax/policy-basics-where-do-our-state-tax-dollars-go.

2. Richard D. Kahlenberg, "How Higher Education Funding Shortchanges Community Colleges," The Century Foundation, May 28, 2015, https://tcf.org/content/report/how-higher-education-funding-shortchanges-community-colleges/?agreed=1.

3. Kenneth Megan, Shai Akabas, and Jake Varn, *Higher Education Trends: Rising Costs, Stagnant Outcomes, State Initiatives* (Washington, DC: Bipartisan Policy Center, March 2017).

4. It also emphasizes the need for the community colleges to refresh the EIS results at the very least every other year. The data sets used to generate the EIS measures change every year and results based on old data are far less convincing. It should become a matter of regular and formal routine for the colleges to do this.

5. Emsi EIS database

6. Ibid.

7. Ibid.

8. CNBC, "Free College Is Now a Reality in Nearly 20 States," CNBC.com, March 18, 2019, https://www.cnbc.com/2019/03/12/free-college-now-a-reality-in-these-states.html.

9. Bob Luebke, "Why Free College Tuition Is a Bad Idea," Civitas Institute, February 4, 2016, https://www.nccivitas.org/2016/16909/.

10. Economic Modeling Specialists International, *Demonstrating the Value of America's Community Colleges, Analysis of the Economic Impact and Return on Investment of Education*, January 2014.

11. David Hudson, "The President Proposes to Make Community College Free for Responsible Students for 2 Years," The White House, January 18, 2015, https://obamawhitehouse.archives.gov/blog/2015/01/08/president-proposes-make-community-college-free-responsible-students-2-years.

12. Ibid.

13. One counterargument is that we are comparing students who do not go to college to students who go to college because they are subsidized. The subsidized students enter lower, but still better jobs than had they not gone to college. The GRP will always increase because now the workforce will be more educated, even if only marginally. What we really care about is whether taxpayer ROI will still be above threshold levels given the massive subsidies of the "free community college" movement. This is doubtful. For the student ROI the only cost we are looking at is opportunity cost so even if they see very low increases in earnings, their ROIs are almost guaranteed to be positive.

14. Bryan Douglas Caplan, *The Case Against Education* (Princeton, NJ and Oxford: Princeton University Press, 2018).

15. Another nuance that may be brought up in this context is student demand. A college can offer a program that may even result in higher occupational earnings, but that doesn't mean that students will enroll in that program. Enrollment projections are a politicized topic for higher-education institutions.

16. David Henderson, "A Pareto-Optimal Move," Econlib.org, *EconLog*, October 27, 2008, https://www.econlib.org/archives/2008/10/a_pareto-optima.html.

17. Some colleges have an "Office of Student Retentions" motivated to retain students who would be better off leaving higher education because it constitutes a huge misallocation of resources. What is good for the goose (the college) isn't necessarily good for the gander (the student). The EIS does not address this moral hazard, or perverse incentive problem. The college president, however, should be mindful of this hazard and use the understanding of the EIS to advance the student placement objective, if that is the preferred pathway.

6

LEVERAGING THE EIS

Program Changes

THE ISSUES

This is how most community colleges are processing the EIS:

- A need to communicate the college's value is brought to attention, an EIS is proposed.
- The box is checked by contracting for an EIS.
- Four months later the results are available.
- A press conference follows where the results are disseminated.
- The college moves on to tackle what are deemed to be other matters, perceived to be *unrelated* to the EIS.

The ideal scenario, of course, is to allow the EIS to become instrumental in how the colleges intend to resolve these matters, i.e., explicitly making them *related* to the EIS. This can only strengthen how colleges engage in the battle for public funding between sectors. Some colleges do precisely this, but they are few. An EIS is typically regarded as just one of many discrete activities the colleges fund during the year; leveraging it to address other issues is unfortunately a rare occurrence.

So, herein lies the opportunity. The EIS is all about the economic activity in the *region* and the college's role in safeguarding and growing it—a much broader topic than just the college itself. The more the region thrives, the better. The regional citizens (and voters) know this, and the community colleges—being significant economic players—are very much in the thick of it. And that's why it is a huge opportunity, not only for the college president to become a leader in all things related to economic development, but also to assume the role of walking in the legislators' shoes, an idea introduced in earlier chapters. Legislators want to ensure that the regional citizens are better off now than when they began their tenure. And a big part of being better off is to be *economically* better off.

So, to do this effectively, college presidents must have a clear appreciation for the legislators' plight in their representation of the taxpayers. The absence of such an appreciation leads to missed opportunities. Legislators are accountable to the taxpayers. College presidents, on the other hand, are accountable to their colleges, but also to the regions they serve. They often advocate for their colleges only, however, without connecting the dots between the requests made for funding and the effects those requests may have on the taxpayers' wallets. Or, perhaps more succinctly, the effects those requests may have on the other public sectors competing for the funding.

Fights over available scarce resources can quickly reach an impasse when arguments made by the college are based solely on the college's needs and aspirations. The arguments made should be a lot more expansive and include the transparency of what the funding requests will actually buy. The *taxpayers' wallets* should be front and center in the college presidents' minds. The EIS data and results could, in this sense, become the rallying point for accountability in managing public monies.

College presidents do battle with many different issues throughout the year. While the EIS results are a necessary tool in these battles, they are not sufficient. The presidents' success in resolving the issues to the betterment of the region served is dependent only on the extent to which *others* are doing their part in pitching in to resolve them. The "others" include the economic development councils (EDCs), the workforce development boards (WDBs), the state and federal governments, and regional industry leaders. College presidents are in a key position to become leaders in this loosely defined consortium.

What specifically then, can the colleges do to advance the cause of regional economic development?

One answer: change the program mix.

The common denominator as far as the colleges are concerned is the economic impact that the changes in the program mix will have on the region. *All* responses to any issue will invariably have cost and benefits components and so, the college should address them while using the EIS databases, model, and results to their fullest. Anything short of that would be tantamount to opportunities forgone.

Several issues can be addressed with targeted changes in the programming at the colleges. Among the major issues that are always in the news (and discussed in this chapter), we have:

- the imbalance between the supply and demand for skills in the workforce,
- lowering the default rate on student loans by increasing the ability to repay loans, and
- countering the typical low completion rates at community colleges.

All community colleges have been affected by these issues in one way or another. The academic and vocational programs are the heart and soul of the colleges. They are the vehicle preparing the students for their careers in the workforce, or for transfers to four-year colleges where they complete their studies and *then* are released to the workforce.

These three issues, however, must be placed in their proper context to understand that targeted program changes can only provide partial solutions. We still have steep uphill battles to fight. Higher-education institutions do not have the stellar reputation they once had.

First—probably the most important one—the colleges are no longer adequately meeting the demands for workforce skills. Even if they have sufficient funding, they only get a "C" grade in prioritizing how those funds are allocated. We can tinker all we want with the programs and make *some* progress, but we cannot focus on that alone. To *solve* the problem, the colleges need to accommodate far more students, and for that they need a lot more funding. They don't need more funding per student, but they need it in total to accommodate more students if any progress toward meeting the skills gaps is to be met. That increase in the number of students is based on increasing the workforce participation rate—an issue that has dominated the workforce news for several years. More on this later.

Second, the colleges are no longer perceived in the media as being *the* institutions that provide the surefire assurance that higher earnings are just around the corner. Our EIS results, however, have been consistently strong and well above threshold levels, so this cannot be entirely true. What *is* true is that education rewards students *less* than it did some decades ago when the focus was more on preparing students for real jobs that paid well.

What we have now is a myriad of culturally in-vogue programs cropping up everywhere, which do not necessarily translate into well-paid occupations in the workforce. The average increase in earnings—the rewards of education—for an entire student body as a result of the education received may, therefore, be *shallower* than the increases experienced before, but still higher with education than without it. So, we stipulate that the higher-education industry has this shortcoming and that the EIS results would improve by changing the program mix.

The program mix, nevertheless, should be the point of attack for community colleges to address certain issues. It defines what the college is all about, its character, and its value to the community as an economic engine. The program mix also reveals if the colleges lean toward the placement or retention objectives. If the leaning is toward maximizing the placement of students in jobs, it means the college is offering a program mix that probably caters more to the specific needs of the regional employers—and that generally translates to a higher economic value. In this case, however, the program mix may include more *difficult* courses that are harder to complete, because employers want specific skill sets that are more technical in nature. These courses are typically associated with an above-average dropout rate. The tradeoff is that fewer students in this college make it through, though they are paid much more when entering the workforce.

If, on the other hand, the strategy is to keep the students in school instead of prematurely dropping out or stopping out, that program mix is likely to include more basic preparatory courses that focus on transferring students to four-year universities, or relatively fewer difficult-to-complete courses and a higher-than-average number of easier courses. The result is fewer dropouts and stop-outs—the students tend to remain in school for the duration more so than in many other colleges. The tradeoff is that they are paid far less when entering the workforce—at least students who do not transfer to four-year universities—and that translates to a lower economic value to the region.

It is an artful balancing act to maintain a program mix that fairly accommodates both objectives. The balancing act is that tweaking or replacing programs is a complicated process, and college presidents must be well prepared for both the political *and* economic consequences. Whenever they make program changes or attempt to disturb the status quo, consequences for political and economic well-being in the region unfold. But disturbing the status quo is necessary, and college leaders must prioritize which among the issues is the most acute, and why. The questions are not *whether* they should respond, but rather, how aggressively they should respond, and how the public square will react?

How they *should* respond, of course, is through the most readily available means to them—the program mix. The programs are *the* reason why the students are enrolling (at least they should be), because they are the means through which students advance to jobs or transfer to four-year universities. How the college leaders' response will be accepted in the public square depends on how well they communicate the economic impacts the proposed changes in the program mix will have. Our contention is that presenting credible measures of how changes in the program mix will have an impact on the GRP and the investment analysis results constitutes the very best response possible.

It all begins with the allocation of a fixed budget. Resources are not unlimited, and so the college leaders must prioritize. Obviously, the issues that keep them on the alert cannot be addressed with program tweaks of *all* programs each year, but *some* are probably way overdue. So, to be practical, we must prioritize which programs to add, cut, or tweak, and know the reasons why we chose this particular order of priority.

The least painful choice would be to continue with the status quo, particularly if last year's EIS results were strong. Not rocking the boat is easy: all we have to do stay under the radar and to ask for only a modest increase in the baseline funding for the operation and maintenance of, say, 120 programs in a given year.

But the political realities are unavoidable. Perhaps this year there is a flurry of prominent articles and TV coverage that tell essentially the same stories (always it seems with a journalistic emphasis on the extreme and anecdotal cases) that community colleges do not do their jobs. The bottom line is that we have to do something. The learned journalists say (as if reading from a script) that the imbalance between the supply and demand for skills in the workforce is growing, the default rate on student loans is also growing for lack of attention by the college leaders, or the community colleges fail miserably in graduating enough students with associate degrees or certificates.

College education is overrated, they say, and not as economically beneficial for the region, students, or taxpayers as has been claimed in the past. The negative press goes on, and no community college president can avoid the political fallout. As these political realities surface for whatever reason, they wear on the college leaders to the point where visible action becomes necessary and sometimes urgent. They must step up with more substantive attention to the problems—and that is never an easy task.

Substantive attention no longer means that the problems are "resolved" with op-ed pieces in the regional press. This is no longer effective. College leaders must keep track and carefully build their case as they respond, including documenting the process of preparing responses from beginning to end. And that begins with the allocation of the fixed budget between departments and programs. Decisions must be made, and priorities established.

The first order of business is to determine which among the 120 programs offered by the college should be seriously tweaked up or down, cut or replaced. Suppose that number is five—we have enough wiggle room in the budget to take a hard look at five programs. Next year, depending on the intensity of the issues then, perhaps a different submix of programs could be selected for closer scrutiny.

A second part of the due diligence is to leverage the EIS results by estimating all the costs and all the benefits of the changes envisioned and simulating them in the EIS model to determine how the result would have changed. This is the simple "what-if" analysis discussed earlier.

Third and finally, the results of the analysis should be presented to the regional stakeholders to begin the process of building momentum in favor of adopting the changes. That momentum is possible only if the EIS results and databases are available.

THE IMBALANCE BETWEEN SUPPLY AND DEMAND FOR WORKFORCE SKILLS

The imbalance between supply and demand for workforce skills in the United States is a huge problem—one not likely to be solved with just changing the program mix of community colleges. It is the *umbrella* concern that bothers us the most—all other issues are less important than this one.

The solutions, however, are elusive because the complexities that bar us from effectively bridging the gaps are overwhelming. They need not be complex, but they are because of the politics involved. Obviously, the community colleges alone cannot solve them—universities as well as the state and federal government must also do their part. And that's where it all falls apart.

States and the federal government maintain counterproductive policies in effect because they have constituencies who hold that *other* reasons—why we have those policies in the first place—trump the economic ones. That is blatantly obvious when looking at the adequacy of community college funding over the years. States and the federal government have not adequately funded the community colleges to even begin to address the problem of the imbalance of the workforce skills in the United States in any meaningful way, even if the colleges in unison achieved perfect alignment of the program mix with the specific needs of the workforce. The problem is overwhelming and calls for an entire paradigm change in the way this issue is handled.

Why is this so? Simply because the current (and fluctuating) level of state public support of the community colleges is *constituent*-driven, and the constituents are represented by the state legislators. The prevailing mood is that taxpayers generally vote no on any kind of public investment, community colleges included. The battles for taxpayer money will always be there, and the likelihood is that they will become increasingly contentious. In the end, the community colleges will always be at the mercy of the vicissitudes of the taxpayers' willingness to support them and left with fixed budgets that can only accommodate a fixed number of students. This is like death and taxes—they are absolute certainties.

Given the inadequacies of the budgets to solve the problem, we are not stemming the tide, but are losing ground. As of this writing, there were 13.4 million job postings in the United States in December 2018 but only 5.1 million community college graduates across programs for 2017—the entire year—to fill them.[1] The demand outstrips the supply by quite a margin. And that's only based on today's low labor-force participation rate (the number of working age people 16 years of age and over looking for a job) of 63 percent. The supply-and-demand imbalance would be a lot worse if the participation is closer to where it should be when it reached its highest level in year 2000, 67.3 percent.[2]

As we can all agree, the low 63 percent labor force participation rate should *not* be the new normal. Yet, we rejoice if we only have a small and fractional increase. We need to do a lot better. In the quest for more funding, community colleges should be at the cutting edge of this issue in lobbying for setting a political target to reach the year 2000 labor-force participation rate of 67.3 percent (shown in table 6.1). This would actually be a modest target compared to many countries where the labor-force participation rate is higher. The United Kingdom, for example, currently has a 79 percent labor-force participation rate. The United States ranks a distant 10th among developed countries.[3]

Community college leaders need to be fully aware of the nuances of the workforce participation rate and understand its role in actually solving the economic development problem in the United States. It begins with the skills gaps in each and every region served by community colleges, and it ends with colleges filling those gaps with both quality programs that respond to the needs of the workforce and budgets to accommodate literally millions more students (but not of the kind that "free" community colleges would bring). The skills gaps in each region certainly could be addressed with program changes, and they should.

The community colleges need to always be aware of ways to improve their program offering in order to meet the regional demands for skills. A much bigger challenge is to meet those same needs if the political

Table 6.1. Labor-Force Participation Rate

Total labor force eligibility	163,240,000
Not in labor force	96,500,000
Officially counted as unemployed	6,294,000
Target participation rate	67.3%

Source: Trading Economics, United States Labor-Force Participation Rate

motivation to greatly increase the workforce participation rate were to be miraculously allowed to flourish. It would mean that many other sectors of the economy as controlled by the state and federal governments would be affected, and that is obviously outside the control of the community colleges.

How big is this problem, and which other sectors would be involved? As of this writing, there are approximately 96.5 million working-age people in the United States (out of 163 million eligible workers) who no longer participate in the workforce—they are not looking for work anymore because their current skills no longer fit with the new skills required.[4] They may have actively sought employment for several months, or years, but have given up, accelerating the decrease in the civilian labor-force-participation rate over time to the low of 63 percent in 2018.

So, what would a target of increasing the labor-force participation rate to 67.3 percent mean for the community colleges? They certainly would become key players in making this happen, and so they *should* be enthusiastically on board. In practical terms, it would mean they would have to equip an additional 4.2 million workers with appropriate training and education that would land them good-paying jobs, as shown in table 6.2. These 4.2 million workers are able-bodied workers, currently unemployed, but who need to become productive members of the workforce.

The *failure* to add these workers to the nation's gainfully employed workforce means that the unemployment numbers are a lot worse than the officially reported unemployment of 3.9 percent. It actually is 6.4 percent, to be exact.[5]

The college enthusiasm for such an aggressive target would soon dampen, however, unless several changes in other areas were also implemented concurrently. But these changes are outside of the colleges' control. They are dependent on state and federal government action, probably a formidable task to say the least. Lobbying for the needed changes must begin somewhere, and why not the community colleges? They will become the *key* actors in making it all happen anyway and so, they should take the lead. Our recommendation, therefore, is to nominate the community colleges as the aggressive lobbyists to build the political will and make the needed changes to resolve the imbalance issue.

Table 6.2. Calculated Results

Actual labor force (LF) participation rate	63.0%
Target LF participation rate	67.3%
Difference	4.3%
% official unemployment rate	3.9
Additional unemployment relative to LF participation target	4.2 million
Total unemployed relative to target LF participation target	10.5 million
Actual unemployment rate	6.4%

Source: US Department of Labor, BLS, "Labor Force Statistics," data extracted January 15, 2019

The first (and most important) order of business to take care of is the declining trend of state financial support as the main culprit for the failure to bridge the gaps. If there is any hope of ever reducing the imbalance between supply and demand for workforce numbers and skills, community college budgets must increase. This, above all, must be communicated in the context of not only bridging the current skills gaps given the low labor-force-participation rate, but also the larger gaps attributable to whatever *target* labor-force-participation rate we set. This is very different from business as usual—advocating for only the colleges' needs and aspirations. Not only will it shift the perspective from the college to the taxpayer, it will also focus on bridging the immediate imbalance between the supply and demand for workforce skills *as only a step* toward increasing the labor-force participation rate as well.

Over the long run, the hope is that this kind of lobbying by the community college leaders will take root with state and federal legislators, who will, ever so slowly, begin to loosen the purse strings. This needs to happen so that the large influx of new students into the community college system can be accommodated with new infrastructure capacity.[6] The economic wisdom of the vision should go a long way in convincing legislators who hesitate to join in. At the very least, they will be held accountable during the reelection season for their inaction.

Second, if miraculously the state governments do their part and the budgets increase (again, not per student, but to accommodate a large influx of new students), the colleges must be prepared to abandon the practice of only tinkering at the edges. Henceforth they must pursue radical changes in the program mix to become more responsive to employers' needs for specific skills. Unemployed workers who have been out of the workforce for a long time often have outdated skill sets and will need retraining to qualify for the current needs of the workforce. The colleges must learn to quickly adapt and to greatly increase the *pace* of change. To train and educate the huge influx of additional workers over a relatively short time period would be an impossible task under the present higher-education system—a complete paradigm switch in how it operates must happen.

Third, not only must the state and federal government increase their funding of the colleges, they must also change the US welfare policies as well. This would entail *disincentivizing eligible workers from choosing to remain unemployed.* Under the current system, some eligible workers have a powerful incentive to remain unemployed because what government programs pay them in food stamps and/or other welfare benefits is more generous than the wages of many of the jobs offered. The gap between the skills needed and the colleges' abilities to fill them will widen unless this situation changes. It is a politically sensitive problem that is most difficult to undo—the political will just is not there . . . yet.

College leaders must be acutely aware of this problem and have it front and center in their lobbying portfolio. The current imbalance between supply and demand in the workforce requires more comprehensive solutions than the temporary fixes they can do on their own. Therefore, they must become the *thought leaders and lobbyists* to the legislators. Change will still come very slowly, however, because it is mired in disentangling the politics, and that will take time.

But our prediction is that the ship will turn ever so slowly if the colleges adopt a much broader focus and lobby accordingly. Enticing students to enroll in programs for which there is little workforce demand or the wages are low just to fill the empty seats is not the answer. Instead, the focus should be on lobbying to *remove* the incentives to remaining unemployed, while promoting programs that will provide eligible workers with an incentive to leave their unemployment status. This is essentially the definition of being a *champion for the taxpayers.*

College leaders are definitely poised to assume a leadership role in making the needed changes a reality. The economic well-being of their regions should be uppermost in their minds; they should lobby for it and give state and federal legislators reasons to respond positively. Colleges should not wait for slow government changes before their part begins—they need to be aggressively proactive now. The government's lack of political will to adequately address the skills-gap problem does not absolve college leaders from still doing what they can. Awareness of the problem is the start, and lobbying for its solution is continuous. Colleges should propose specific interventions and conduct a "what-if" analysis to measure the extent to which stopgap solutions will increase the GRP. Everything college leaders do to advance this cause must fit in with the broader vision of increasing the workforce participation rate to close the supply-and-demand gaps in the workforce so that *taxpayers*, not just the college, will be better off in the end.

So, this is the process by which the colleges move closer to the production possibilities frontier, even though these actions in the aggregate will not *solve* the imbalance problem. The long-term *objective* is to build a strong case for budgetary increases using data-driven arguments. If the request for budget increases fails, plan B is to provide the background justification for a *shift* in the fixed budget by expanding some programs and/or adding new programs while cutting others.

Plan B, however, is fraught with regional political consequences, at least under the current system. Any time cutting entire programs is proposed, or drastically changing the materials taught in existing programs (which may render the old faculty incapable of teaching the new materials required by the employers), there *will be* political consequences—winners who rejoice and losers who become vocal in the public square.

Tinkering at the edges with only minor tweaks to avoid the political battles is no longer an option, however, given the magnitude of the supply/demand skills-imbalance problem. College presidents must become a lot bolder in proposing major changes to the program mix on a regular basis to ensure that the needed skills are supplied at a reasonable cost. That's the ideal, and it will require that the programs are designed to be supple in their capacity to accommodate changes fast.

Cutting programs is never easy, particularly if they have served local companies well over the years. All politics are local, as the saying goes, and situations often arise when the question becomes real: should a college prioritize local needs in their program planning, or do regional or statewide needs trump the local ones? In a zero-sum game, if there is an increase here, there must be a corresponding decrease elsewhere.

Suppose local employers have benefited from the existence of the college's welding program for years, but are ignorant of the fact that although welding occupations may trend upward locally, the opposite may be true regionally or statewide. The college may have satisfied the local demand for trained welders for some of these employers and are in their good graces, but now the data shows that the demand for welders in the broader region and statewide is actually declining, and wages are stagnating. In fact, were it not for the strong demand for welders from one large local company, welding as a long-term career option holds little promise. (Note that this is not an attempt to dissuade welders, it is merely a hypothetical example used to illustrate a point.) The college president is therefore faced with a hard decision. Should the welding program be cut even if the local demand is still strong? If so, the ire of the local employer will also be very vocal in the local press.

Clearly a change is needed, but to what? The budget is still fixed, and the college cannot continue to allocate scarce dollars to maintain a program that may be stagnating, even though all of the graduates do get jobs the moment they become certified. What should the welding program be replaced with?

Suppose there are three sizable manufacturing companies in the college's region some distance away from the college in dire need of 100 well-paid machinists per year for at least the next 15 years due to impending retirement of the older workers. The demand for machinists is even stronger because other nearby regions have similar workforce shortages. Besides that, no nearby community colleges offer a machinist program of the kind needed. This information alone will considerably increase the probability of success of a new machinist program at the college.

Anticipating this move, the college leadership initiates discussions with the employers about the interest in launching a new machinist program. Over time, the college leadership gains the confidence that the creation of such a program would be the right decision. The immediate challenge is to determine which program to cut (again, remember that the allocation of funding between programs is a zero-sum game). The three remaining tasks at this point before a hard funding request is made during the legislative session are:

- to confirm that the move—adding a machinist program and cutting the welding program—will increase the GRP, given the successful achievement of the next two bullet points;[7]
- to minimize the local political fallout associated with cutting the welding program; and
- to incorporate in the analysis the cultural reason why the companies have difficulties in filling the 100 positions every year.

The reason for the last bullet is to reiterate the point made earlier—that older workers who are parents of community college-age kids tend, more often than not, to discourage their sons or daughters from going into the jobs they are about to vacate. It is not uncommon for them to say they want their offspring to have a better working career than they had had, so they push for them to become a doctor, lawyer, or something more "white collar" and prestigious. How to incorporate this in the analysis is through the higher costs of recruiting and accommodating more students into a program and enduring a higher dropout rate.

When the due diligence of the proposed move is rigorous, it *will* account for the cultural nuances of the impending change in the program mix, and also the fact that the new program may be academically more difficult to complete. Following the path of least resistance as most do more often than not, many students enrolled will drop out and enter something easier as soon as they encounter academic difficulties. The level of overall academic challenge required to strike an optimal balance between students landing high-paying jobs through the new program and, at the same time, reaching an acceptable retention rate must be taken into account.

Only by making the appropriate conservative assumptions in the analysis is when it measures whether the gains outweigh the losses. And, if the gains outweigh the losses after this kind of analysis (i.e., the GRP would increase), then the decision in favor of cutting welding and replacing it with a new program is eminently justified. It is all about allocating scarce resources most efficiently, *and* maximizing the regional economic well-being. These are the political and economic realities college presidents face. They cannot satisfy all constituencies at the same time.

To summarize, the college proposes in the legislative session to cut the welding program and replace it with a new machinist program where graduates are offered a stronger probability to gain regional employment as well as higher wages. The gains from that move will be greater than the losses. The numbers show this. The political fallout from the local employers, therefore, will be minimized or blunted because it will be met with cogent and data-driven arguments.

At a minimum, this new and much more prominent role for the college leaders in safeguarding the economic well-being of their regions requires that they become experts on the regional labor market and the industries and companies that dominate it. This entails an up-to-date knowledge of the:

- regional economic base;
- regional demographics (population, gender, education levels, ages, the occupations in the workforce, and the statistics on how many workers in each occupation are close to retirement);
- regional industries and occupations, the rates at which they have grown or declined over the past several years, and forecasts of how they will grow or decline in the future; and
- regional companies at risk of closing down or being offshored.

These bullet points are the "raw materials" for determining the validity and relevance of the programs the college *should* offer to be in the good graces of the regional employers. Clearly, the regional industries and companies exhibiting a declining influence on the regional economy should, all else being equal, be served less by the college program mix than industries and companies exhibiting robust growth, unless there are compelling reasons to the contrary.

Community colleges are *dependent* on the regional employers and the geographical regions they serve. They depend on the regions for most of their students and for the taxpayers who fund them. How well the community colleges serve the regional stakeholders, or react to impending calamities or opportunities in the region, in part explains why some companies choose to leave the region, or stay. All regions are always at some risk of losing vital companies or industries because they find better business environments elsewhere. The probability of that happening, to a large extent, depends on how well the colleges monitor the economic health of the region and how well they act to stave off impending calamities, such as: (a) alleviating regional skill shortages, and (b) replacing older workers as they retire. The former involves the colleges' willingness to change the program mix to provide the right skills for the regional employers. The latter is to simply expand existing programs so that more qualified workers are available to replace those retiring out of the workforce. Both are vitally necessary.

So, why are some regions at risk?

Five words: skill shortages and corporate taxes.[8]

The skill shortages are in the community colleges' wheelhouse. They can do something about these through economic analyses of program changes to measure how much the regional economic well-being will be affected. The corporate taxes, however, are a different issue. Here, the community college leaders, in the quest to safeguard the regional economic well-being, should be very much aware of this issue and become active lobbyists to ensure that companies at risk stay in the region. The skill-gap issue should be accommodated directly through interacting with the companies themselves—meeting their specific needs for skills. For the tax issue, the college leaders should join these companies in lobbying for the removal of tax structures that are unnecessarily unfavorable to business.

Both are needed, and community college leaders should be intimately involved in finding solutions. Companies that are more at risk for leaving need attention, and college leaders should do everything they can to safeguard *the college's existence*, which depends very much on the counterpart existence of a thriving business community that hires their graduates.

The skills shortages, exacerbated by the low labor-force participation rate as described above, demonstrably hurt the US economy, and companies are naturally anxious about the near-future status and quality of the workforce. Qualified workers are not only in scarce supply, the few made available are too expensive because so many companies compete for them. It becomes difficult, therefore, to compete in the international marketplace. The result is that many companies, rather than invest in on-the-job-training of American workers, locate offshore, where the skills are available for less.

Offshoring has been a real problem for decades, and we have been losing the battle. Colleges have been sluggish in responding to the workforce skill needs in both quality and quantity because they are not receiving anywhere near sufficient funding to allow them expand and/or tweak the programs offered to add the number of workers with the right skills needed. The new normal for colleges is that doing anything but the status quo, or merely tinkering at the edges, comes with a good dose of both economic and political pain, and that is to be avoided. But a lack of, or only tepid, action by the community colleges to alleviate the acute regional needs only greases the skids of an exodus of businesses from regions not acutely aware of these problems.

"Manufacturing used to be a larger component of the U.S. economy. In 1970, it was 24.3 percent of GDP, double what it was in 2018," says personal finance website *The Balance*.[9] Today, little is truly manufactured in the United States. Chances are that whichever product *claims* to have been manufactured in the United States, actually means it was only assembled here. The component parts were, in all probability, manufactured overseas somewhere. It is possible, however, that the exodus of companies could have been slowed down significantly if the community colleges had been: (a) proactive in their responses when the signs of the workforce skills imbalance first appeared, and (b) actively and successfully lobbied for competitive corporate taxes for companies at risk. It is not too late to start now, however, to prevent further erosion.

It should be clear from this discussion that college leaders need to be a lot more vigilant in monitoring the health of the regional economy than they ever were before. No one should be taken by surprise. Community colleges should be in the thick of all this, because they are major economic players, if not the most important players, in the regions they serve. As part of this vigilance, they need at a minimum to *establish and nurture* much stronger working relationships with the regional companies, the EDCs, and the WDBs than they have in the past. More importantly (and to reiterate), the colleges should assume the *leadership role* in developing comprehensive economic growth strategies for their regions. The very fact that they have recently completed the EIS makes them all the more eligible to assume that leadership role by virtue of the fact that they now have access to all the regional data curated in ways that permits the assessment of economic impacts of proposed actions intended to benefit the region.

A leadership role begins, at a minimum, with serving on the boards of the EDCs and WDBs to participate in the coordination of their activities to:

- protect and serve the current economic base of the region,
- identify and court new companies into the region for the purpose of filling the supply-chain needs of the primary companies,
- focus on meeting specific skill demands of key regional companies, and
- be willing to change the program mixes to align with all of the above, including the EDCs and WDBs.

One major risk of the colleges' *not* doing any of this but instead only reacting tepidly to the regional calamities (such as companies leaving overnight) as they occur is this: when primary companies leave the region, the nearby supply chains are likely to leave next. These (supply chain) companies depend on the primary company for their business. Therefore, when the primary leaves, they naturally will be at risk too. For any region, a primary company choosing to move away either offshore or to an entirely different location in the United States will probably be economically disastrous for that region, particularly a rural region. It becomes very difficult to repatriate the same industries once they have left.

It is far better to take action *before* the companies leave, not to simply *react* to the situation after they have left. The actions include knowing what a skilled workforce needs and preparing to meet those needs, filling the gaps of a defective supply chain, ensuring that the wages of the graduating students remain competitive, and a friendly-to-business tax structure.

All of these ingredients should be very much inside the community college wheelhouse, either directly as they relate to the quantity and quality of the regional workforce, or indirectly as they relate to lobbying for a tax structure that is fair to corporations. The ingredients are all vitally necessary, and they must be supplied concurrently to safeguard the regional economic base and to trigger any kind of significant regional economic growth.

Given the many nuances of the problem, labeled here as the "imbalance between the supply and demand for workforce skills," the colleges should seize the opportunity to do a lot more than just react to whatever the EDCs, WDBs, and/or the regional companies decide to do, or not do. They need to be much more proactive in their regional communities and to take the lead in the strategic development of the region.

The program changes are an important part of the process, but they are only a small part. The regional strategic development must be comprehensive and present a united front from all of the experts and stakeholders, and the community colleges should be on top of the food chain.

The structure to ideally put in place is that college leaders, as leaders in regional economic development, leverage the collaboration with other regional stakeholders (EDCs and WDBs) to effectively stave off companies from uprooting and weakening the regional economic base. This will consist of streamlining the activities of the stakeholders to minimize overlap or redundancies, maintaining lists of companies at risk of leaving, and keeping an eye on the economic health of the supply chains and specific workforce skill needs. With this structure in place, the economic health of the region will be front and center and the stakeholders will be proactive *in a unified fashion*, rather than reactive. They will address the problems up front—before they happen—not after they have already happened.

All the stakeholders should ideally be on the same page in any region. When they are, small changes can trigger big political wins. The absence of this collaborative spirit essentially means that the local EDCs, WDBs, and other regional stakeholders would point their fingers at each other and the local community college to straighten up *their* act. After all, it is not their fault that the region suffers from deficient economic development; they are doing their individual part, the fault always lies elsewhere.

Now, however, with the ideal collaborative spirit in place, the solutions proposed should be a lot more comprehensive, and directly involve the other actors as well. Changing the program mix at the college is very much an important part of the solution, but so is the EDC's work in identifying the regional companies at risk and their supply chains, and the joint work needed to stave off any impending moves. The WDB's work with the community college is also very important in making sure that their programs are complementary to the college proposals, and to help ensure that funding for the program changes at the college is forthcoming. A college president advocating alone for his or her college is less effective than if joined by advocates from the WDBs, the EDCs, and other stakeholders as well.

To summarize—the problem for a college president is not *only* about the college's funding needs that will allow it to operate (the alpha and omega of the past), it is now much more about the comprehensive economic well-being of the entire region. And *that* requires active involvement by *all* of the regional stakeholders. The collaborative spirit in all of this can only be generated if there is a dynamic leader who takes the reins and charts the direction.

That leader should come from the community college for two reasons: (a) the college is likely to be among the top economic players in the region (as clearly shown by the EIS results) and, as such, (b) their proposed actions are the most visible and also the most doable in the quest to reduce the imbalance between supply and demand for workforce skills. The EDCs and WDBs can provide some programmatic support, but the community college deals with the heart of the matter—the quantity and quality of the regional workforce—the main preoccupation for a company's decision to stay or leave.

The recommended process is presented in the following four steps.

Step 1: Conduct PDGA with Regional Employers

The first step in the process of addressing the problem is to confirm that there is, indeed, a regional imbalance between the supply and demand for workforce skills in the regional economy and how wide it is. This is carried out by way of a program demand gap analysis (PDGA)—a simple and formal way of confirming, with data, that the gaps exist and in what magnitudes.

We now have our proverbial ducks lined up.

The PDGA provides data-driven measurements of the supply of graduates from the college (*and* neighboring colleges) to compare with the regional demand for those workers reflected by the number of regional job openings.

Where there are gaps, obviously there are also opportunities, which must be analyzed more in depth. The EDCs and WDBs, firmly on board with this step, would also benefit greatly from the results of such a study because their approaches to solving the problems for the region would be much better focused. Knowing the specific nature and magnitudes of the gaps will allow them to structure their programs so as to maximize the benefits to the regional companies when actions are taken to close the gaps.

The direct beneficiaries of these actions—the regional companies and industries—should also agree with this first step. As members of the regional economic development consortium, their inclination is to make things work. Usually, they prefer to stay in the region rather than leave. In that context, it makes economic sense for them to deepen the relationship with the community college, even to the point of agreeing to provide some specific help for the colleges in the forms of direct financial support or in-kind technical equipment.

Employers are willing to *invest* in the quality and quantity of their own labor force—this is easily observed by their costly outlays in competing for skilled workers. Many colleges, however, have not yet realized that the *burden is on them* to convince the employers that there is ample opportunity for them to actually make those investments in the college, in dollars, or in equipment that the college can use to train workers with the specific skills that the employers need.

Employers should sweeten the agreements with the colleges by offering to provide them support of the targeted program, either in the form of equipment (machinery, etc.) to be used for teaching, or funding support, in exchange for getting the first right of refusal for, say, the top 15 graduates out of that program. The 15 would then have guaranteed well-paying jobs at the end of their academic careers, and the remaining graduates would have increased their chances for employment in other companies with similar workforce needs nearby. This will incentivize the students to stay with the programs and overcome any academic difficulties that may arise.

Finally, the agreements between employers and the colleges should include specific actions to reduce the stigma of a "blue collar" label by pointing to career pathway opportunities *beyond* that particular occupation within the company, including earnings. This is a problem that puts filling jobs, even high-paying ones, into context. The "blue collar" label associated with many occupations is a real problem that takes a lot of diplomacy and cajoling to overcome in the college-program recruiting process.

In a nutshell, the problem is that parents of college-age sons and daughters have visions for their offspring to move into careers better than they themselves are about to retire from. And so they tend to be reluctant to help support their offspring in their enthusiasm for a blue-collar career pathway.

Step 2: Determine Why the Gaps Exists

Having confirmed with the PDGA that the gaps exist, the second step is to find out *why* they exist. Obviously, some companies are identified as at risk because they are unhappy with the low number of workers coming out of the community college, *and* those workers' level of preparedness. They have to spend much more to import qualified workers from outside the region (or to train an unqualified workforce from inside the region), and that just has to change. Furthermore, the rumors are rampant that these companies are thinking about leaving the region.

Although the community college may have been aware of this problem, their hands have also been tied for years. The college has had budgets to only accommodate 100 students in the affected programs while the PDGA showed that a minimum of 250 are needed. Thus, the college was not the *reason* for failing to fill the gap; the real reason was that the budget was never sufficient to fill it.

Step 3: Undertake the Analysis

With the PDGA in hand we have the evidence needed to justify a request for an increase in funding in order to increase the capacity of these programs to serve more students. Step 3 is to undertake the analysis to determine the return on investment (ROI) of the proposed project to change the program mix and whether those returns are sufficient to justify the request for increased funding. The analysis includes what it will cost to build the program's capacity and what the benefits will be. If the present value of the latter exceeds the former and they meet or exceed the threshold values, the proposal is feasible and the change in the program mix is economically justified. The PDGA determines *where* there are gaps and how wide they are, and the EIS model and databases help determine the costs and benefits of filling them.

Step 4: Submit Proposal for Funding

Having completed the above three steps, we are now ready for step 4—submit the proposal for funding.

Two realities now unfold.

One is to ask (with the backing of the employers themselves, EDCs, WDBs, and other economic development stakeholders), for a funding increase for a simple expansion of, for example, two existing programs to meet a documented demand for regional workforce skills, while requests for funding for everything else is on par with last year's funding. The second one—the more likely reality—is that although legislators may heartily agree with the proposed changes, their hands are tied. There is only so much money to go around. This is all political speak of asking the college to make room in their program mix to accommodate the expansion of the two target programs, i.e., cut some programs.

If the EDC, WDB, and college consortium lobbying for the first option succeeds, there will be some political fallout. One will be the usual lamenting of property tax losses as the college may have to expand its infrastructure to accommodate the larger influx of students. Another one is statewide—the politics of sorting out the zero-sum game in the higher-education sector (who would gain) and the other sectors also funded by the state (who would lose or be cut back). Nothing is easy when battling over scarce public resources—the expansion of the two programs still involves a request for more money for the college, and that will have to come from somewhere.

So, if the first scenario fails, cutting some programs is on the table. In this case, the simple fact is that *now* the program chopping block becomes real for other programs that do not show similar economic potential as the two programs to be expanded. A comprehensive PDGA also identifies at-risk programs at the college—the ones that contribute less to the gross regional product (GRP).[10] These programs become the short list of candidates that could be marked for elimination. It is here where the rubber meets the road and where the local politics come into play—the selection of which programs to cut and why and justifying the decisions with data of the kind that only the EIS databases can provide.

To conclude this discussion of the imbalance between supply and demand for workforce skills, simple *awareness* by college presidents of the importance of this phenomenon, and what they can do about it, is half the battle. The broader problem should bother them, even though no rapid government changes that would facilitate addressing them (such as loosening the purse strings) can be expected. Awareness of the shortcomings of the existing (and inadequate) system and all its complexities is needed "fodder" for lobbying aggressively for changes to be made. But to become effective lobbyists and to lead a consortium of the economic development actors in a region, the college leaders need to be fully aware of the local, regional, and national problems in need of solutions. All the actors must be formally on the same page before they can begin to address the gaps.

DEFAULT RATE ON STUDENT LOANS

The high default rate on student loans by community college students is an issue of great concern to many college presidents, albeit a smaller issue than just previously discussed. It has been prominent in the higher-education news for several years because it carries dire consequences for the affected colleges if not addressed head-on.[11] Many colleges are at risk of losing all federal aid if the default rate reaches or exceeds 30 percent for three consecutive years. The average default rate for all public community colleges within a three-year period is 17 percent, which means that several colleges find themselves on the far to the right end of the bell curve where they hover just south of the 30 percent threshold. If the students from these colleges cross that default threshold and federal funding is cut entirely, that would be the financial kiss of death. Colleges with a 40 percent default rate in a single year can lose federal aid immediately.[12]

How significant is this problem? Well, in 2016, in the higher-education sector alone, "42.4 million Americans owed $1.3 trillion in federal student loans. More than 4.2 million borrowers were in default as of the end of 2016, up from 3.6 million in 2015" according to a Consumer Federation of America analysis of US Department of Education data.[13] On average, more than 3,000 borrowers default on their federal student loans every day. People who default on their student loans "are going to have a tougher time passing an employment verification check, saving for retirement or ever buying a home," and "borrowers in default can also have their wages garnished and their tax funds seized."[14]

Community colleges are certainly prone to be affected by this problem because they serve students from the lower tier on the family earnings scale more so than the universities. Community college leaders, therefore, must address this problem more aggressively as the default rate keeps getting incrementally worse over time. Many colleges are at risk of reaching the point of seriously flirting with the federal funding cut-off threshold level.

So how do these colleges *actually* address this problem? Many will hire financial counselors to work directly with the students likely to default, and establish in-house offices to deploy sophisticated tracking systems that explicitly deal with at-risk students. These approaches are certainly necessary, but not sufficient, certainly not if that is the sum and substance of the response. They are far less potent than if proactive solutions are taken, such as changing the program mix with a view to increasing the average earnings of the student body. Colleges will need to estimate the costs of offering new programs, estimate the benefits, and present the full package to the legislators for funding as a comprehensive solution to the problem.

As more students move to higher-paying occupations when they leave colleges, it eventually begets a lower default rate on student loans. That only makes logical sense—higher-paying jobs will have the effect of increasing the ability to pay back loans. This will reduce the default rate over time to the point where the issue will no longer be a politically sensitive one in the media. Because the fix is in and it is working, the issue will no longer rise to the top as most politically visible in need of urgent attention. The measures of: (a) the extent to which the changes in the program mix will add to the GRP and (b) how the students and taxpayers are affected are an added bonus generating regional goodwill as the political negativity this issue typically brings is lessened.

The four steps outlined in the previous section applies here as well, although the messaging will be different because the issue is different. When the issue is the default rate on student loans, the message to resolve it should change accordingly. The PDGA must still be done to confirm that an increase in the number of students in some programs is indeed warranted. If the results confirm the skill shortages, then we proceed with the analysis and cost out the changes to be made.

Suppose that the cost estimate to accomplish this amounts to $600,000, including the infrastructure needed to accommodate an increase in the number of students and the additional faculty and staff needed. We then simulate how much of an impact this change would have by simply plugging the changed numbers into the EIS model to trace through how this would change the results. Through this process, if we find that the GRP will likely rise by $1.5 million as a result of implementing this proposal, the request for the funding increase of $600,000, therefore, is eminently worthwhile from a legislator/taxpayer perspective.[15]

At the conclusion of the analysis, we will know that the proposed action is economically feasible and justifies the requested increase in the budget over and beyond the funding level of those programs last year. We will also know that the loan default rate will be reduced and will conduct the marketing campaign accordingly. The reason for the proposed change in the program mix is to reduce the default rate on student loans. As we then move more people into higher-paying jobs, the marketable logic is that higher earnings beget an increase in the capacity to repay the loans.

Finally, and to add another dimension to the marketing campaign, we will be able to show that the changes in the program mix will allocate scarce resources more efficiently. This is not only because the revised results say so, but also because the proposed changes will be more responsive to the local and regional employers. In the end, when all of the above is carefully documented and communicated to the stakeholders, only a small change in the program mix can have a significant political upside. Mission accomplished. Two political wins with one strike—higher GRP and more efficient allocation of resources—would be difficult for any legislator to deny.

LOW GRADUATION OR COMPLETION RATES

The results from having conducted some 2,000 EISs so far reveal a much maligned and, to many, surprising statistic: only an average of 4.6 percent of the students enrolled during the analysis year complete their one-year certificates, and only an average of 8.3 percent complete their associate degrees.[16] These are low numbers. Actually, only 5 percent of community college students earn their associate degrees in two years, while 36 percent of four-year private and flagship public university students earn their bachelor's degrees in four years. That percentage drops to 19 percent at nonflagship four-year public universities."[17] It *is* a problem.

The political impetus for community college leaders is to launch actions to increase the graduation rates because the issue has received so much bad press in the national and regional media. Almost universally, the media portrays the community colleges, in particular, as doing a poor job retaining students in school. Too many students drop out, they lament, and something needs to be done.

But as said before, the devil is in the details. The media makes no distinction between dropouts and stop-outs, nor does it account for the fact that the community colleges must fund the remedial training of non-college-ready students who have supposedly "graduated" from the high schools. This all affects the graduation statistics. The stop-outs often return to *eventually* complete their education. It takes them a bit longer, but many of them do complete. That is not necessarily a bad thing, it only signals to the marketplace that the community college is flexible enough to accommodate these students. These students choose to remain in college *until they get a good job*, then they stop out. While in their new jobs, most of them will enjoy higher earnings from having attended college for *some* time, even though they did not graduate. They have amassed some of the skills needed for the job, but not all of them. So, turn this around—make this a rightfully *good* argument for the community colleges.

The coverage of this issue is definitely not a good reflection of the media because only half of the truth is told—the proverbial fake news—at least when it comes to the community colleges. The other half is the good news about the two-year colleges, that they are supple enough to accommodate students of *all* stripes, not only those who seek academic degrees and have no other legitimate barriers to complete their careers as students. Community colleges can accommodate students who stop out and take interim jobs, noncredit students who do not seek degrees, and students who need remedial training and take a long time to complete their studies. Nevertheless, college presidents who did not get that memo tend to ignore effective communication of the other legitimate reasons why the graduation rates are as low as they are. The community colleges were *designed* that way. They are *supposed* to be different. Their *customers* are different. It is a messy system, but somehow it works. Those stories need to be told a lot more forcefully.

Turning bad perceptions into good ones, however, is only nascent—the bad perception of low graduation rates persists. Telling the other half of the stories only blunts the political realities some. The problem is in sorting it all out—not an easy task at all. The community colleges must understand the demands they are supposed to meet are of a wide variety. Not only do they serve a wide diversity in student profiles, there is an equally wide variety in goals pursued—a lot of them nonacademic. There is also the constant demand for workers from employers who recruit students away from the colleges prematurely. Because of this, the graduation statistics for the student body as a whole will suffer accordingly.

Would the world be better off if the community colleges were not created to meet all of these different demands? The answer is obviously no. The dominant perception, however, is that higher education is supposed to be orderly, and when graduation rates are low, then the colleges are at fault. Many colleges react to *what should be good news* as if they are guilty and promise to do better. How they react is embracing the political argument of how bad it is to have low completion rates while ignoring the reasons why they exist in the first place.

Which brings us back to the program mix and what colleges can do to remedy this problem. It is a *balancing act*. We should always strive to move toward the production possibilities frontier to find the most efficient allocation of resources. But we must first establish the overall strategy, which trajectory—placement or retention—we would like to be on. These are widely different strategies, and they require different program mixes. The balancing act in selecting the program mix is the art of optimally blending the following several important considerations:

Strategic trajectory. Which strategic trajectory—increased placement, or retention—will be the least politically volatile? While choosing the least or most volatile strategy, or somewhere in between, college leaders will have a sense of the political fallout that is in store for them as a consequence of their choice, and be prepared for it.

Inputs from the regional employers. Will the skills needed by the regional employers warrant the tweaking of, or creating entirely new programs? This describes the intensity of the proposed change and how it will translate into realistic cost estimates.

The degree of difficulty of courses in the proposed mix. Will the degree of difficulty of courses within each tweaked or new program sufficiently accommodate the strategic trajectory, and where on the scale of higher earnings for the students will the revised program mix be located?

Impact of the regional economic well-being. Will each change in the program mix have a positive impact on the GRP?

Striking an optimal balance depends on the college's ability to message the changes. And in turn, that depends on the political itch, or where it is apparent that attention is most needed. If the message is based only on anecdotes, it will not likely succeed. If, however, it is based on credible data and advances the economic activities in the region, then chances are much better that it will succeed.

CONCLUSION

As discussed in this chapter, while the issues may require solutions in the same form, i.e., program-mix changes, the *messaging* will be different. If the current political itch is the imbalance between supply and demand for workforce skills, the message must be more expansive and originate with the *consortium* of partners in economic development—the colleges, EDCs, WDBs, and the regional companies. Presenting a comprehensive united front to the decision makers increases the likelihood of getting the funding needed to proceed. A comprehensive and united front also includes what the *government* must do to make the changes effective. From the college's perspective, its limited role is to change the programs in order to be more responsive to the employers' needs.

If the current political itch is the high default rate on student loans, the messaging should be from primarily the community college and the regional employers. After lengthy discussions, the colleges and the employers agree that the college should change the program mix to be more responsive to the employers' specific skill needs. If needed, the college may have to cut some programs to make room for the new ones.

That message should be the extent to which the regional economy will improve as a result of making *all* the changes.

If the current political itch is a low completion rates, the message from the community college should be that, indeed, it *is* a problem, and it needs to be addressed. Everyone agrees that the completion rate should be higher. The other half of the story, however, needs to be told as well. There are solid reasons why the completion rates are low, although they should not be used as convenient excuses. Perhaps the college has suffered an unusually high dropout rate because the courses are too difficult. Or perhaps the stop-out rate has been high because students with only one or two semesters under their belts have been snapped up by employers. It all depends on what is happening in the regional economy and how that affects the low graduation or completion rates. It really is *not* about the college's ability to retain students, even though there are staff dedicated to that very purpose by hiring a bunch of counselors to convince the students at risk to stay in school. Rather, what is happening in the regional economy is far more influential in the college's enrollment.

The *reasons* for the existence of all of the issues discussed need to be far better communicated to the stakeholders by the college leaders. Presently, these issues are perceived by the media as negatives for the community colleges, whereas they, in fact, should be regarded as positives. Changing the program mix should be accompanied by tempered, but different, messages that balance out the need to fill the skills gaps, reduce the default rate on student loans, and get the retention rate up, with the suppleness of the colleges to accommodate a wide diversity of students to get an education *their* way. That message will blunt the political negativity of this phenomenon.

NOTES

1. From the Emsi Analyst software. Of course, postings for the same job may appear several times, but not this lopsided—comparing job postings (demand) for one month to qualified workers exiting college (supply) for an entire year.

2. Trading Economics, "United States Labor Force Participation Rate," 2019, https://tradingeconomics.com/united-states/labor-force-participation-rate.

3. Ibid.

4. Actually, this statement is perhaps bold because the 96.5 million figure includes stay-at-home moms who, obviously, are not actively seeking work because they prefer to raise their children at home.

5. US Department of Labor, Bureau of Labor Statistics website, "Labor Force Statistics," bls.gov, data extracted January 15, 2019.

6. This, of course, assumes that the colleges are at capacity now, and a large influx of new students will require additional infrastructure capacity to accommodate them. Indeed, several colleges already have excess capacity and an influx of additional students can be accommodated without any additional infrastructure capacity. The point of this discussion, however, is that if the political will changes to increase the workforce participation rate, there will be substantial increases in costs, some attributable to added infrastructure capacity, some just to accommodate larger student bodies.

7. To add some complexity to this, it is entirely possible that the GRP in the local region—the one the college serves—increases but the GRP in the state decreases as a result of the program change. The scope of services requested for this added analysis should include this nuance.

8. Obviously, the five words: "skill shortages and corporate taxes" only apply to larger towns or cities that have an economic base with some variety of regional development options available. There are literally thousands of incorporated small towns or communities in the United States that fall below the radar here because there are no realistic options available to practice state-of-the-art regional economic development.

9. Kimberly Amadeo, "US Manufacturing, Statistics and Outlook," *The Balance*, January 5, 2019, https://www.thebalance.com/u-s-manufacturing-what-it-is-statistics-and-outlook-3305575.

10. The Emsi model does not actually measure the programs that contribute less to the GRP. We do, however, measure programs that are producing more graduates than there are annual openings or jobs in the region. Graduates of those programs end up being underemployed or must improve their skill set to get decent jobs, or they leave the region to get jobs that use their education.

11. Collin Binkley, "DeVos Warns of Crisis Amid Ballooning Student Debt," Associated Press, November 27, 2018, https://www.apnews.com/383f53f0cbb2439792f9ffcd06ce196e; Jason D. Delisle, "The Left Gives Community Colleges Another Free Pass for Unpaid Student Loans," AEI, August 29, 2018, http://www.aei.org/publication/the-left-gives-community-colleges-another-free-pass-for-unpaid-student-loans/.

12. Andrew Kreighbaum, "GAO: Colleges, Consultants Game Rules to Lower Default Rates," *Inside Higher Ed*, April 27, 2018, https://

www.insidehighered.com/news/2018/04/27/gao-finds-colleges-manipulating-loan-default-rates-keep-access-federal-aid.

13. Consumer Federation of America, "More Than 1 Million Federal Student Loan Defaults in 2016," press release, March 14, 2017, https://consumerfed.org/press_release/new-data-1-1-million-federal-student-loan-defaults-2016/.

14. Tom Anderson, "More Than 1.1 Million Borrowers Defaulted on Their Federal Student Loans Last Year," CNBC Personal Finance, March 14, 2017, https://www.cnbc.com/2017/03/14/more-than-11-million-borrowers-defaulted-on-their-federal-student-loans-last-year.html.

15. This holds even if the taxpayer ROI goes down as a result of the change so long as the decline in the ROI does not go below the threshold level.

16. Economic Modeling Specialists International, *Demonstrating the Value of America's Community Colleges, Analysis of the Economic Impact and Return on Investment of Education*, January 2014.

17. Jon Marcus, "Colleges Confront the Simple Math That Keeps Students from Graduation on Time," *The Hechinger Report*, February 17, 2016, https://hechingerreport.org/colleges-confront-the-simple-math-that-keeps-students-from-graduating-on-time/.

7

LEVERAGING THE EIS

Nonprogram Changes

Program changes are the easiest and fastest ways for community colleges to *do* something rather than just talking about fixing the issues. In this chapter, we introduce some issues that cannot be addressed directly through program changes. These include: (a) tuition rates and their effects on overall enrollment; (b) remedial training, so often lamented as a problem by community college leaders, and for some states; (c) whether it makes economic sense to annex districts for taxing purposes.

As discussed in the previous chapter, changes in the program mix are perceived to partially solve many problems, and that is accompanied by mostly political upsides. Perception counts, and whatever colleges do to remedy problems must be accompanied by the marketing messages that hit the right key. The specific program-change actions taken by the colleges are reflections of what the colleges can do given fixed budgets—just about the only thing the colleges *can* do to allocate resources more efficiently.

The above-mentioned issues, however, cannot be easily solved with program changes. Instead, they require that college leaders have some fundamental knowledge of economic principles and the ability to effectively apply them. This small subset of issues is briefly discussed below.

TUITION AND ENROLLMENT

Emsi's aggregate economic impact study for all community colleges in the United States (2014), showed a total enrollment of 11.6 million academic credit students, excluding all noncredit students.[1] For the privilege of attending a community college, the average student spent roughly $882 in tuition and fees, which bought him or her an average of 14 credit hours' worth of education. This (the mother of all averages) is simply the total enrollment divided into the total amount of tuition and fees collected by the colleges.[2]

Of course, this begs the question that should be asked of all community college leaders: is an enrollment of 11.6 million academic students too high, or too low? The beginning of at least a partial answer is found in the calculated tuition rate—the average of $882 in this case.

The first thing college leaders must know is that the tuition rate does, indeed, affect enrollment. A high rate means that fewer than the optimal number of students are enrolled. The prescription would be to decrease the rate and the number of students enrolling would increase. If, however, the average of $882 per student is too low, the reverse holds. The rate should then be increased so that enrollment would decrease below the 11.6 million students. The sweet spot is when the tuition rate generates an optimal number of students enrolled, consistent with when the revenues for the colleges are maximized.

This is the workings of the simple economic theory of the *price elasticity of demand*.

The price elasticity of demand should reside in the consciousness of any college president so that the right tuition rate and enrollment decisions are made given the budgetary constraints imposed on them by the legislators. High prices (tuition and fees) beget fewer students, and low prices beget more students.

The lower the price the more we tend to buy—students will flock to the college.

The higher the price the less we tend to buy—potential students will not enroll.

An optimal number of students enrolled would maximize revenues for the colleges.

But here's the dilemma. College presidents always want more students. It is essentially a one-way street because more students mean higher funding from the state and/or the federal governments—this is baked into the state funding formulas, and to a large extent the federal funding formula as well. The presidents also fully realize that enrollment varies with the strength of the economy. When the economy is strong, enrollment goes down because people choose to work rather than go to school—jobs are plentiful. When the economy is down, the reverse happens. Those enrollment swings are natural.

What is not natural is when enrollment is down because the college failed to do something about it. Few college leaders are adept at turning the political tide to the colleges' advantage and avoid looking guilty in serving too many or too few students. For that, it is important to "weaponize" some key knowledge of economic theory, such as the price elasticity of demand. At the same time, the college should develop a well-tailored marketing message that shows the economic rationality of *not* always following the conventional wisdom, which is to increase tuition to fill the impending state funding shortages so that *at least* the revenues collected are not declining relative to last year.

And this brings us full circle to the price elasticity of demand and to the 11.6 million student headcount. In the aggregate economic impact study (EIS), we used an average estimate of –0.04 as the overall estimate of the price elasticity of demand based on a composite of elasticity measures found in the literature.[3] For every 10 percent increase in tuition, the enrollment would decrease by 4 percent.[4]

Here's the problem—the elasticity measures change between regions. In some regions it may even be elastic whereby a 10 percent increase in tuition and fees will cause a *more* than 10 percent decrease in enrollment. In other regions, the responsiveness to price changes may be highly inelastic, more so than the average estimate used of –0.04, and so a price increase of a 10 percent magnitude would only trigger a less than 4 percent drop in enrollment. The smaller enrollment multiplied by the substantially higher price would cause total revenues to increase beyond what it was the year before. So, all of this raises the question—should the quest be for more students or more revenues? This is a balancing act.

College leaders should be keenly aware of the specific estimate for their region. It would be unwise to increase the price in some regions because *total revenues* would fall from an even greater increase in student enrollment. It depends.

Simply put, the price elasticity of demand measures the "degree of responsiveness of the quantity demanded of education (enrollment) to changes in the market price (tuition and fees). If a decrease in tuition and fees increases total revenues, demand is elastic. If it decreases total revenues, demand is inelastic. If total revenues remain the same, the elasticity of demand is unitary."[5]

If we multiply the average rate of $882 per student in tuition and fees by the student population of 11.6 million, we derive a total revenue stream of some $10.2 billion nationwide, or roughly 16 percent of all revenues generated by the colleges.[6] Applying the average elasticity measure of –0.04 means that a 10 percent increase in tuition—to $970—would cause total revenues from tuition to increase from $10.2 billion to $10.8 billion, or a reduced student body of 11.1 million multiplied by $970 increases total revenues to $10.8 million. If, however, the elasticity measure for the nation as a whole had been an *elastic* –1.1 percent, then the reverse would be true. A 10 percent increase in tuition—to $970—would cause total revenues to *decrease* from $10.2 billion to $10 billion (a reduced student body of 10.3 million multiplied by $970 decreases total revenues to $10 billion).

Here is where the balancing act comes in. The revenues from tuition and fees comprise only roughly 16 percent of the total revenues generated by community colleges. The other sources of revenues are local (property taxes) and state appropriation (a combined total of 55 percent), federal revenues (17 percent), and all other revenues (13 percent).[7] These revenue sources are all connected to the student enrollment. The more students, the higher the financial support from both the state (appropriations and property taxes) and federal sources (Pell and Perkins).

So, even when the price elasticity of demand is inelastic and raising tuition will increase the tuition revenues, it is not always economically wise to do so. Colleges will soon see a corresponding drop in revenues generated from the other sources as the student headcount drops, perhaps even more than the extent to which tuition revenues increase. So, the quest is to find where the sweet spot *is* when raising the tuition that will not unduly trigger a disproportionate drop in support from the other sources. And finding that sweet spot begins with the knowledge of what the price elasticity of demand is for the individual colleges and their respective regions.

If tuition is entirely "free" (as it would be under the "free" community college momentum—see chapter 5), then the enrollment will increase significantly as students will flock to the colleges to take advantage of the subsidies, whether or not the education offered there is the prime motivator. Or, if the tuition is very high, only a few students would enroll and the school would eventually have to shut its doors. It is a balancing act to find the optimal number of students served. That number is derived when the tuition rate increases (or decreases) to the point where the marginal cost of serving the students equals the marginal revenue.

So, enrollment is governed to a significant extent by the price elasticity of demand. There *is* an equilibrium tuition rate which balances the supply of students with the demand so that just the right number of students enroll without being artificially incentivized. The aggregate estimate of –0.04 used in the Emsi aggregate study for all the community colleges in the United States means that the average price elasticity of demand is *inelastic*, on average. If the price elasticity of demand is measured at –0.04, then a price increase of $100 will lead to a drop in enrollment of only 4 percent. If the price elasticity measure is unitary, a $100 increase in price would lead to a drop in enrollment of 10 percent. A price elasticity of –1.1 (elastic) would mean that a $100 increase in price would lead to a corresponding drop in enrollment of 11 percent. All of these different elasticity measure would generate large differences in total revenues.

The average estimate of –0.04 means that, for some colleges, the price elasticity is more inelastic than –0.04 and for others it may be even extending into the elastic range of the curve. It is different between regions and college leaders should do their due diligence of determining where on that range their particular college is.

To do so, however, is difficult at best because there is not a lot of research done on the price elasticity of demand for community colleges. But to know the importance of the role it plays, and to make an assumption about it, are crucial. The solution is not always to offset a budgetary cut through state appropriations by increasing tuition and fees. There are limits, and many moving parts will change as a result of such action. Knowing by how much a price *could be* increased while not unduly affecting the revenues from tuition and fees *and* the other revenue sources is key. Again, it is a balancing act.

The price elasticity assumption needs to be as realistic as possible because it dictates the outcome of a price change. In this context it is useful to look at the more voluminous research on this phenomenon for public four-year universities in particular. Any price elasticity estimate for community college enrollment is probably more sensitive to a $100 tuition price increase than are the estimates for private or public four-year universities. This should come as no surprise because, on average, community college students tend to come from a lower family-income background and because of this, are more price sensitive. The range for the average effect that a $100 tuition increase would have on enrollment (as implied by these papers for public four-year universities) is –0.023 to –0.074, hence our middle-of-the-road estimate of –0.04 for the community colleges.[8]

Our recommendation is to use this average estimate as the baseline. The college (probably the Institutional Research department) could then do the research on the region's demographics, its economic base, and the tuition rates of other colleges and universities located in that region, and use this to generate an elasticity estimate that either moves further into the inelastic range or toward the elastic range. In turn, the proposed change in the tuition will either increase or decrease the total revenues after adjusting for the enrollment based on the price elasticity estimate used.

So, from the elasticity estimate we get the change in enrollment and eventually how the revenues generated will be affected. Straightforward. But, alas, it gets just a bit more complicated. We still have to correlate all of this with the state or federal funding formulas.

It is entirely possible that an estimated decrease in enrollment resulting from a tuition increase will trigger state or federal funding formulas so that a proposed tuition hike is rendered moot in terms of revenues generated. In such cases, it would be wise to raise tuition only to the point where the changing enrollment does not trigger any change in the state and federal funding formulas. The endgame is to finely calibrate what the tuition change *should* be, or finding that sweet spot where the decrease in total revenues collected is minimized, or decreased as shallowly as possible in response to a cut in state funding.

To bring us back to leveraging the EIS, the following is a hypothetical illustration of the impact on gross regional product (GRP) that may occur when the college decides to shift the funding burden to the

LEVERAGING THE EIS

students by increasing the tuition and fees in the face of reduced support from the state taxpayers. Table 7.1 summarizes the analysis.

Suppose the current enrollment at the college is 12,000 students who are supported by state and local government (property taxes) to the tune of $4,000 per student. The rumors are that state support is due for a decline, and so the college leaders are proposing to increase the tuition and fees by 10 percent to offset this assumed decline in state funding support. The IR department has done its due diligence and determined that the price elasticity of demand is an inelastic –0.04, or a 10 percent increase in tuition will trigger a 4 percent decrease in enrollment.

The current level of enrollment will, because of this price elasticity, decline to 11,520 students if the tuition is increased to $1,100 per student (10 percent). State and local government's annual funding support declines therefore by nearly $2 million, to $46,080,000. And, so do annual benefits—they decline by $2.8 million because 480 fewer students will enroll and eventually enter the workforce.

The good news is that the taxpayers will pay less, $1,920,000 to be exact. But for every dollar state and local governments save (due to increased tuition payments and reduced enrollments), they also lose an estimated $2,800,000 because fewer students will enroll, or a net de-

Table 7.1. Reduced State Support and Increased Tuition

Current Situation	
Enrollment	12,000
State and local government funding @ $4,000/student	$48,000,000
Tuition revenues @ $1,000/student	$12,000,000
State and local government benefits	$70,000,000
Shifted burden scenario, elasticity	–4%
Enrollment (after), losing 480 students	11,520
State and local government funding @ $4,000/student	$46,080,000
Tuition revenues after 10% hike @ $1,100/student	$12,672,000
State and local government benefits	$67,600,000
Comparison	
Change in state and local government support	–$1,920,000
Change is state and local government benefits	–$2,400,000
Net change in regional GRP	–$880,000

crease of $880,000 in GRP. The fiscal condition of state and local government is made worse by the funding shift, and a tax increase or other revenue enhancement would be needed just to break even.

When it all shakes out, we have more than $1.9 million to make up in lost revenues to remain revenue neutral. By increasing the tuition by 10 percent, we also increased the tuition revenues from $12 million to $12.67 million, so we got part of the way to make up the lost $1.9 million—but only 35 percent. We still have 65 percent to go. This, however, is the best we can do if the regional elasticity estimate is the correct one. A more inelastic estimate, say –2%, will generate a different result—a 10 percent tuition hike will get us 98 percent of the way to revenue neutrality. Due diligence of the regional price elasticity of demand, therefore, is very important.

The impact on revenues aside, however, the political argument to be made is the fact that the regional economy *will* be negatively impacted by the looming budget cuts. The legislators should know this, *and* the numbers. They should not be able to simply assume that the problem of college funding goes away *because* the tuition is increased and that this bridges the shortfall. It doesn't work that way, and the legislators need to be informed of this fact.

The other aspect about the enrollment issue is a more difficult one to navigate for the colleges—whether public funding of higher education in general is warranted. The perception among many is that the taxpayers' funding of higher education is way too high. Some say no taxpayer money should go to higher education—the students should pay it all—but most say enough is enough, any further significant increases are not warranted.

Economists have mixed reactions—it is an issue that needs to be debated and this little book will not endorse a particular side of this issue. Milton Friedman, Adam Smith, Gary Becker, and John Stuart Mill are a few among the notable economists who favor public support for higher education because of the additional benefits it brings society in general. We have also confirmed this phenomenon by the nearly 2,000 economic impact studies we have conducted: education pays—in general. The present value of all costs is lower than the present value of the benefits.

However, we also recognize that the benefits are *shallower* than they would be because many students enroll in popular "in-vogue" programs that do not lead to high earnings in the workforce, therefore resources have been allocated inefficiently. Gender studies come to mind—they may be interesting to many, but they do not translate into solid job opportunities in the workforce.

Connecting the dots between the resources made available to the colleges and the size of the regional GRP, the resources *would* be allocated more efficiently if these "in-vogue" programs were cut and replaced with programs much better aligned with the workforce needs. There are lots of possible improvements to be made, and there should always be an urgency front and center to move closer to the production possibilities frontier.

The mere existence of relatively easy-to-complete and "in-vogue" programs increases enrollment probably beyond its optimal point. Offering subsidies, easy-to-access student loan programs, and serving remedial students also affect enrollment. All of these affect the EIS results, which are still well above threshold levels. That's the system we have now and what the taxpayers are asked to support. What it tells us is that there is a lot of wiggle room to do things badly before the EIS investment analysis results move below the threshold levels.

So, given the inefficiencies "the system" now permits, and given the current dissatisfaction with the system as expressed by taxpayers, what should we do about the rising perception in the public square of whether continued public funding of higher education at all is warranted? To answer that question, we should separate the issues to clarify why public support of higher education may still be economically warranted, while always working diligently to remove any inefficiencies.

Suppose we had a choice between serving 1,000 unsubsidized students attending a community college under a perfect (unsubsidized) allocation of resources, or 1,000 unsubsidized students plus 500 subsidized students attending because lower (subsidized) tuition rates made it possible for the additional students to attend. The latter choice reflects the current situation—the well-off students pay their full tuition, and the not so-well-off students are subsidized with lower tuition rates through grants or other means to allow them to attend. So far so good. But any system that allows for subsidies will be taken advantage of. It depends where the subsidy cutoff point is.

If subsidies are readily available to everyone, schools could be inundated by students who have little business being in college in the first place. Furthermore, they are the ones who increase the demand for the many programs currently offered at the colleges that have few prospects for employability. This is the grounds for taxpayer opposition. They are waking up to this reality, and many taxpayers feel that college is not something that warrants their financial support.

The fundamental question is whether a larger number of students (the 1,500 in this case) earning more money, paying more in taxes, ending up in jail less, having improved health habits, and so on grows the economy more than the loss attributable to the initial inefficient allocation of resources that allowed the additional 500 students to attend in the first place. Subsidizing in this sense (through financial aid and other mechanisms), and/or offering "easy" programs that do not lead to jobs or higher earnings may not be a bad economic deal for society at large. Strictly speaking, however, it remains an inefficient allocation of resources because the EIS results are not as high as they ought to be, yet they are still well above threshold levels.

Having an additional 500 students attend because of subsidies is a misallocation of resources. These students, who otherwise could not go to college, now do, and so enrollment (demand) increases, with the result that colleges generally increase their tuition rates. More students increase demand, and therefore, the average price per student will increase as well. In addition, as enrollment increases, the infrastructure too becomes strained, which increases the demand for yet more public aid to grow the college, and so the spiral continues.

In another sense, however, the fact that students who otherwise could not attend are able to attend college also means that many externalities occur, impacts that would not otherwise be there. These 500 additional students, on average, make more money *because* of their education, although not nearly by as much if they had pursued more rigorous academic objectives and landed better and more high-paying jobs. They pay more in taxes, they go to jail less, they draw unemployment and are on welfare less, and so on. Add all of this up, and the overall economy may be stronger as a bottom-line measure than had they not attended, despite the fact that resources may have been misallocated.[9]

What does all of this mean for college presidents? It simply means they need to be *aware*. Increasing the tuition in anticipation of impending budget cuts is not as easy as it once used to be. They need to be aware of the price elasticity of demand for their region and the calibration to be done on tuition hikes given the public (state and federal) funding formulas. They also need to be aware of the rising discontent among taxpayers for an ever-increasing demand for higher public funding of higher education institutions (of course with the exception of those taxpayers who want "free" community colleges).

And all of the above means the colleges should never lose sight of the quest to move the needle to increase the efficiency of managing the scarce resources made available to them. The imperfections in the marketplace (the existence of programs that do not connect well to the labor market, subsidies, etc.) should be viewed by the college presidents as *temporary* phenomena to always be improved on over the long run. The matching marketing message should make it abundantly clear that they are, indeed, aware and are seeking to maximize the economic well-being of the region, not just the college.

THE REMEDIAL PROBLEM

One way to improve the allocation of scarce taxpayer resources is to use the EIS results to lobby for a reduction in the need for remedial training at the community colleges. Literally thousands of students nationwide receiving their high-school diplomas every year are nowhere near college ready—they need remedial training.[10] What is next for them? In most states, many will enroll at community colleges because the universities will not take them. The universities are not bound by open-access policies, so by default, the only readily available alternative for these students is the community colleges. The costs associated with this policy alone are significant and also an economic deadweight loss if left as is.

The dominant perception among community college leaders is that this is a lost cause. Because the issue is mired in political realities, the perception is that there is little room for the community colleges to successfully argue for an increase in their budgets at the expense of the K–12 sector. And so, they defer. They grudgingly accept the notion of being perpetually held responsible for the remedial training needed. Life goes on, and community colleges dutifully undertake this task, much to the chagrin of the college presidents at every national conference this author has attended.

But even though this is the prevailing reality, having the EIS results in hand does provide a platform for mounting a strong argument on this issue. And that argument may be more effective during the next legislative battles.

So, let's summarize the facts—many students have "completed" their high-school requirements and are contemplating where to go next. Because community colleges are bound by an open-access policy, these students can easily find their home there. The universities are not bound by this policy and so, the community colleges are obliged to cover the cost of bringing these students up to speed for as long as it takes. Next, consider the fact that the EIS results reflect how the portion of available, and scarce, resources were misallocated because they were siphoned off to cover the costs of remedial training. Now imagine how much better the community college results *could be* if these costs were shifted back to the K–12 system where they belong.

Even if only a small part of this problem were resolved through a different funding formula, it alone could substantially increase the taxpayer return on investment (ROI). Despite the fact that a college has to spend a considerable sum of money on remedial training, the taxpayer ROI is still exceeding the threshold level significantly. Think how high it could go if the need for remedial training at the colleges were greatly reduced.

According to the *Washington Post*, "One in four students have to enroll in remedial classes their first year of college, costing their families nearly $1.5 billion, according to a study released by Education Reform Now, a think tank."[11] This is a failure owned entirely by the K–12 system for which the community colleges are made to pay.

When EIS results for the colleges are available, however, the opportunity is there to correct this inefficiency through collective action—all colleges in the state acting in unison. College presidents could mount a forceful economic argument that the GRP would likely improve substantially—from X to Y—if this inefficiency were removed. In a zero-sum game, the "ask" would be for permission to restrict access for the remedial students—they should remain the responsibility of the K–12 sector. The real value of the EIS results here would be to contextualize the colleges' request for financial resources by highlighting the inefficiencies of requiring colleges to accommodate students who are not college-ready.

An example of an opportunity rising out of the remedial training issue is the following. Suppose a state's community colleges requested a total of $1 billion in state funding, and that a total of $50 million of that amount would be spent by the state's community colleges on bringing the remedial students recently graduated from high school up to speed. The college leaders should clearly communicate in their budget request that the $50 million earmarked for spending on remedial training would be a deadweight economic loss because it would delay the onset of the higher earnings for as long as it would take to bring these students up to speed.

Now, suppose further that the college leaders requested that the $1 billion level should remain intact, but *without* the requirement to incur the $50 million worth of remedial training. This would change the picture entirely. The total funding request would not be increased, which should please the legislators, but the $50 million *freed up* could now be spent on students who *are* college-ready, and who would exit the college sooner rather than later to become part of the workforce. This would increase the GRP substantially, and in measurable ways.

How to do this effectively is, unfortunately, more of a political question than it is an economic one—meaning that the measurement of the GRP with and without may not be enough. In many states, the higher GRP argument alone may not be sufficient to shift the remedial training burden back to K–12.[12] Innovative approaches are needed. One such existing program has some potential—the dual-enrollment programs in many states. This may be the ticket. In addition to the obvious economic benefits reflected by any net increase in GRP, legislators in many states are now openly embracing dual-enrollment programs where high-school students receive high-school and college credit simultaneously. It makes sense, legislators argue, because incurring the program cost reduces the time needed before students can become productive members of the workforce. To make it work, legislators typically promote funding initiatives for *both* the K–12 and higher education sectors through the Adult Basic Education (ABE) funding earmark mechanism as an alternative (and speedy) way to earn a GED and college credit.

But (and there is always a but), the dual-credit program is very expensive, yet it is an earmark with lots of political enthusiasm behind it. So, it is an already-existing vehicle that can probably be tweaked to accommodate the remedial training problem. In short, by reallocating a greater portion of the ABE funds to the community colleges only to be earmarked for remedial training, *both* the K–12 and the higher education sectors would still have sufficient resources—albeit a bit tighter—left over to continue with the dual-enrollment programs for qualifying students.

The economic argument here, of course, would hold only if *all* the freed-up resources were devoted to providing education for college-ready students. The student headcount lost from not accepting remedial students (unless ABE funds were made available only to community colleges) would be replaced by other students who *are* college-ready. The K–12 system, on the other hand, would be responsible for denying diploma graduation privileges to students needing remedial training.

ANNEXING TAX DISTRICTS

Finally, we take a brief look at the last issue on the checklist of issues introduced earlier—annexing tax districts. The taxpayers in most states provide funding for the colleges in three ways, either through tax appropriations (earmarks in the state budget), local property taxes, or both. In this section, we are drilling down a bit more into the nuances of local property taxes and how they could drive the taxpayers into political awareness.

Families settle in different locations for different reasons. If they are on the move and have school-age kids, they would typically choose to live in the good school districts and would be willing to pay the higher local taxes there. Empty nesters or families on the move with infants, however, would typically choose to live in districts (or states) where the taxes are lower. And then we have the folks who live all over the place who agree to tax themselves, or not, to support the college. The existence of the college becomes a hot political issue when and if the requests for higher property taxes to fund the college emerge. It is during that crucial time period that college leaders must present elegant economic arguments to turn the perception around from the college draining the pocketbook to actually filling it over the long term.

One opportunity to illustrate this phenomenon is in states (Texas, primarily) where taxing districts and what they fund are an issue. Suppose the taxpayers living in a district not taxed to support a college now find themselves in a political movement to convert their district into a taxed district because so many students from there enroll at the college. Suppose further that the proposal is to ask the taxpayers there to pay an average of $100 more in property taxes per year to support the college. That would increase their property tax burden from an average of, say $1,400 previously, to $1,500 per year. If this were the only information provided, all the taxpayers would know is that their property taxes will increase, and the knee-jerk reaction would be to vehemently oppose it. In these days, the tax burdens are already perceived to be high regardless of what they are. So, it will be very difficult to convince people to increase their own burden to benefit the college.

The missing information is the benefit side—what the additional $100 tax burden will buy. And, this is where the college leaders need to step up their skills in arguing for the proposal—the *benefits* from the taxpayers' perspective of agreeing to tax themselves to fund the college. The task before them is to convince taxpayers in the currently nontaxed districts to vote in favor of the proposal to become a taxed district, for economic reasons. Tax annexation in this sense is a political issue rooted in simple investment analysis. Does it make economic sense for the taxpayers to make this investment?

Here's what the analysis would reveal about what could happen if the proposal is accepted, and the economic arguments that could be made:

- *More* students from the now taxed district will enroll because of the lower tuition rate in accordance with the price responsiveness effect triggered by the lower tuition rate.
- When the students exit the college, most of them will join the workforce in the district they came from, where they will earn substantially more and therefore pay more in taxes.
- By virtue of their education, these students will statistically become better citizens in terms of their social comportment (reduced crime, welfare, and unemployment, and improved health, all correlated to higher levels of education).
- All of these benefits accumulate over time as more students receive their education and join the workforce, and will eventually

fully cover and exceed the costs of the additional $100 increased tax burden.

In return for the taxpayers investing the additional $100 per year to support the college, therefore, suppose that the benefits stream in this hypothetical example adds up to $12 per year for the taxpayer, comprised of the total of increased tax collection from the higher incomes, plus the lower social burden (measured in dollars saved) inflicted on the taxpayer-funded social services. As this benefit stream accumulates and grows over time, the benefits will gradually begin to overtake the $100 investment burden, reach a breakeven point, and then exceed the investment cost allowing real tax benefits to emerge, as shown in figure 7.1 and table 7.2. The taxpayers can expect tax relief beginning in year 9—the crossover point—which grows over time as a result of agreeing to the annexation.

Before annexation we showed in our example that the average tax burden was $1,400 per year. After the annexation, that burden increased by another $100 for a total of $1,500 per year as shown in the first row of the table. Given the assumptions in this hypothetical case, the crossover point between benefits and costs occurs in year 9, fol-

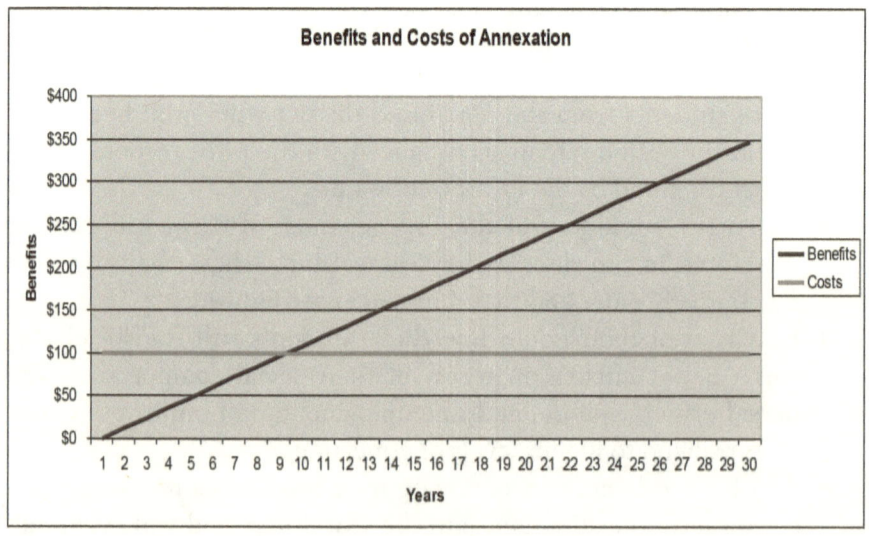

Figure 7.1. Benefits and costs of annexation

Table 7.2. Tax Annexation Cash Flows

Year	Benefits ($)	Taxes		Tax Burden	
		Community College ($)	Other Taxes ($)	$	%
1	0	100	1,400	1,500	107
9	96	100	1,304	1,404	100
30	348	100	1,052	1,152	82

lowed by the continued increase in benefits relative to the constant cost over time.

The "Benefits" column in the table shows the accumulation of benefits over time, growing from $0 in year 1 to $348 in year 30 at a rate of $12 per year. The "CC" column (community college) shows the additional $100 investment made by the taxpayers, and the "Other" column shows the tax burden before annexation. The "Total Tax Burden" columns show the burden after annexation in dollar and percentage terms, beginning in year 1 with $1,500, or an increase of 7 percent. In year 2, however, the tax burden can be reduced to $1,488, or offset by the benefits increase that year—the $12 in the first column. Now, the total tax burden is only 6 percent higher (last column). Beyond year 2, the total tax burden gradually reduces over time until it reaches parity with the preannexation burden of $1,400 between years 9 and 10. Beyond year 10, however, the total tax burden reduces all the way down to $1,152 (82 percent), or far lower than original preannexation burden of $1,400.

The bottom line on all of this is simple: tax annexation will cost the taxpayers slightly more in the short run, in this hypothetical case: by nine years. But as the college adds more skilled workers to the workforce over time, earnings and tax collection will both increase, rendering the state treasury and the taxpayers in better financial shape than would have been the case absent the college; hence, the state can afford to reduce the total tax burden over time and still have enough to pay for all of the services rendered. The taxpayers are indeed better off, in this example, with annexation than without it.

CONCLUSION

The balancing act is more effective when the economic development of a region depends on the concerted effort of several actors. To this end, the colleges must work closely with the economic development councils (EDCs), workforce development boards (WDBs), regional companies, and universities to advance their *joint cause*—which should be to live and operate in a dynamic and thriving community with a well-supplied and skilled workforce in which regional employers are incentivized to stay and employ local residents. All of the stakeholders must be on the same page and do their part. Their common counterparts are the legislators who decide how the available public funding is allocated. Legislators must be lobbied, cajoled, convinced, courted, and held accountable. They all want the same thing—a dynamic and thriving community endowed with a skilled workforce—but they have differences of opinion on how to get there.

In this chapter we have highlighted some areas where the EIS can be leveraged to, at least partially, resolve politically hot issues. The politics differ between regions, as do the community colleges' capacity to deal with them. The EIS *can* be leveraged, however, if we all accept the simple fact that most issues can be expressed in terms of dollars and cents. That acceptance should be equally obvious to all the stakeholders. They should be equally anxious to resolve the issues—whatever they are. If the political focus is on enrollment, then it behooves the college president to fully understand the ramifications of always attempting to compensate for budgetary shortfalls with raising tuition and fees. It affects revenues, and the key is to understand the price elasticity of demand for the region the college serves.

If the issue is the remedial problem, the lobbying to address the problem should be more expansive and involve all the college leaders in a state. Acting collectively, and with solid data-driven economic arguments, should be enough to sway the legislators in their direction. The colleges need to make sure that the due diligence is solid, that the GRP will increase, and that the investment analysis from the perspectives of both the students and the taxpayers will be more attractive.

Finally, if the issue is how to succeed in annexing tax districts—perhaps the most difficult of them all—college leaders should focus more in their messaging on the long-term benefits to the taxpayers than the costs. The added costs are only a short-term phenomenon, soon to be repaid by the cumulative benefits in added tax collections and government savings over time.

NOTES

1. Economic Modeling Specialists International, *Demonstrating the Value of America's Community Colleges*, 2014. For all intents and purposes, this was an aggregate EIS for all community colleges, although IPEDS data was available for only 1,025 colleges.
2. Ibid.
3. The elasticity of –.04 is based on the observed fact that as prices rise, fewer students will enroll, hence the negative sign. Any measure less that –1.0 is labeled as inelastic, a –1.0 measure is labeled unitary elasticity, and any time it exceeds –1.0, the response to enrollment moves into the elastic range, i.e., a 10 percent increase in price triggers a greater than 10 percent drop in the number of students enrolled.
4. Ibid.
5. Ibid.
6. Ibid.
7. Ibid.
8. Christopher J. Molitor, *Price Elasticity of Demand for Community Colleges*, a report prepared for CCbenefits, August 2003.
9. Of course, in a perfect world, the public would be ultimately better off if the taxpayer money were perfectly allocated between sectors; i.e., no subsidies at all. But politics trumps economics, and subsidizing some students for whatever reason is a fact embedded in the system that cannot be easily dislodged.
10. Of course, among the many students who need remedial training we also find significant numbers from the workforce who may have been laid off and who now need retraining. These students may have to be brought up to speed to qualify for the kind of retraining they need.
11. Danielle Douglas-Gabriel, "Remedial Classes Have Become a Hidden Cost of College," *Washington Post*, April 6, 2016, https://www.washingtonpost.com/news/grade-point/wp/2016/04/06/remedial-classes-have-become-a-hidden-cost-of-college/?noredirect=on&utm_term=.edd9de2f2bb7.
12. Of course, shifting the burden of remedial training back to the K–12 system will only shift the costs back to the K–12 institutions, with little net gain to the GRP. The cost increases for K–12 will be offset by the benefit gains for the community colleges. The K–12 system should, however, be responsible for

the college readiness of their student bodies, so the burden is on K–12 to make it happen, not the community colleges.

8

ALTERNATIVE FUNDING SOURCES

So far, we have described what an economic impact study (EIS) is, is not, and how the results can be leveraged to address other issues that college leaders must tackle every day. The good news is that for most colleges, the EIS results are strong and are used with confidence to help secure funding for next year from the traditional sources, mostly from the traditional state appropriations and property tax sources. Those dots are connected, and the simple message to the taxpayers is: "fund us more so we can do more of the same . . . the way we do things works because our impacts are so great." That's the way many colleges use the EIS results.

Our appeal in the previous chapters, however, is to extract a lot more value from the EIS than just the fact that the results are strong. They can also be used as the lifeblood for not only straightforward funding requests, but also in dealing with many other issues, including another dimension—courting alternative sources of funding.

This expanded use of the EIS should become the new normal, but it requires some work. And that work is that college leaders should become familiar with the EIS analytical processes, at least familiar enough to answer basic questions and discuss the conservativeness and soundness of the methodology applied, the meaning of the results, how the results can be improved, and what this means for the state and local taxpayers. The colleges' role in regional economic development needs to become the new mantra with the college leaders—the presidents in particular. They are naturally poised to assume the leadership role among the stakeholders engaged in this new direction.

All of this requires money, because the colleges need it to expand in order to become *the* purveyors of regional economic development—the new trend of education, science, and business that spawns entrepreneurship. This role for the community colleges may be slightly ahead of its time for now, however. States are not getting on board (yet), shown by their unwillingness to provide the funding needed. While there is no doubt that excellent EIS results reflect that education pays, states' funding decision makers have their hands tied. Taxpayers need to change their perception of higher-education institutions and their role in regional economic development, and that takes time.

The willingness of taxpayers to fund ever-increasing demands for resources in the higher-education sector, however, is getting perilously close to maxing out. The taxpayers don't yet understand the true value of higher education. The handwriting is on the wall. The funding of community colleges by state appropriations and property taxes—both significant contributors to college budgets from state taxpayers—have declined steadily over the past 10 years. The Center on Budget and Policy Priorities reports that state spending on public colleges is well below historical levels and that colleges have had to compensate by increasing tuition rates and reducing both faculty and their program offering. The average state spent $1,502 less per student in 2018 than they did in 2008.[1]

This confirms the growing state taxpayer resentment against ever-increasing tax levies over the past several years. Proposals that increase the tax burden, such as bond elections for colleges or school districts, are now more easily met with strong resistance because the impact on the pocketbook is acutely felt through higher property taxes. For community colleges, these battles are gradually being lost because bond elections are rejected more often than they are being embraced.

A significant part of the reason for this decline is that the economic benefits to the taxpayers of supporting the community colleges are not well communicated by the college leaders. The linkages between the investments made by the taxpayers and the returns directly back to those same taxpayers could be made a lot more explicit. The taxpayers and their representatives—the legislators—are, therefore, largely more ignorant of the regional economic importance of the community colleges than they should be. It is incumbent on the college leaders to educate them on this reality so that the momentum of the funding decline would at least slow down, if not stop entirely. As is typical for now, funding decreases happen more often than funding increases.

In the quest to remedy this gradual funding decline, bond elections are often sold flawed, with underestimated costs and overestimated benefits. This, however, becomes a fool's errand in the long run because deceptions (albeit unwitting) will be remembered and haunt the proponents the next time around when other bond elections are proposed. Overselling something with underestimated costs and overestimated benefits will not work in the long run because voters are becoming increasingly sophisticated, with access to more information faster on any issue that will ultimately affect their pocketbooks.

Taxpayers all over the country don't like to pay taxes and tend, more frequently now than before, to vote with gusto *against* most anything that will increase their taxes, and *for* anything that will reduce their taxes, particularly during economically difficult times. Enough is enough. The colleges can do everything right, but the fact still remains that public funds are drying up ever so slowly. It is an uphill battle to educate the taxpayers, and their representatives, on the difference between paying for something without a visible return, and investing in something that actually pays back.

Each year, the level of taxpayer funding for community colleges is uncertain. For now, it is essentially at the mercy of where we are in the business cycle. During good years, requested funding increases are tolerated more easily and initiatives may pass without much political controversy. During economically difficult years, however, taxpayers feel the intrusion of the IRS and the state tax authorities much more acutely, and will vote accordingly.

Lately, there have been more bad years than good ones. Those few who vote with less emotion and who understand that community colleges indeed are the economic engines in the region, which the EIS results confirm, are the kinds of taxpayers we want to increase in numbers. And so, educating the taxpayers to understand the economic role of community colleges—that they add to, not detract from, the economic well-being of a region, that the students and taxpayers are far better off with rather than without the colleges—is paramount, both during good and bad economic years.

The regional economic development benefits of investing in colleges must be personalized, not only briefly mentioned on page 4 in a footnote of the colleges' annual reports. It is about the messaging. The links between investing taxpayer money in the colleges and actually receiving some direct economic benefits in return are dots rarely connected. Which leads to the perception people often have that community colleges are akin to a black hole, a drain, money spent and never to be seen again. This perception should disappear altogether because it has no basis in the truth. The strong regional impact numbers and investment analysis EIS results clearly show that taxpayers are far better off with the colleges than without them.

The bottom line is that we strongly recommend that colleges continue with their strategy of approaching the legislators with the EIS results and with an objective of receiving a bigger slice of each year's fixed budget pie. All else being equal, it should have some traction in favor of the decision on next year's funding level for the colleges.

That's one profitable use of the EIS.

A second one is to apply the same message to an extended audience—the alternative sources of funding—private individuals, foundations, and corporations. Courting alternative funding sources has now become much more of a necessity than it is a luxury or a sideline activity. The more economically literate the college leaders are, the smoother the transition will be to this new normal. It essentially becomes an insurance policy that enables college presidents to expand their horizons from being concerned only about their colleges' welfare to encompass their roles in the much broader arena of regional economic development. The colleges are often the most important economic engines in this arena—we know this because the EIS results tell us so—and thus, they are means to a greater end, not the end themselves. Explicitly recognizing this far more important role for the colleges, budgets should not be unduly constrained by the (now shrinking) availability of public funding. There is much work to do—more workers with the right skills are needed—and this requires looking elsewhere for additional resources. Success with additional funding sources becomes crucial much sooner than later if the colleges are to expand their economic relevance beyond that of only continuing to accommodate students as they have in the past.

ALTERNATIVE FUNDING SOURCES

For now, community colleges are in a very difficult funding situation if they want to play an expanded role in regional economic development, as they should. The colleges need more money in their budgets to meet the increasing demands for:

- training the *regular* students transitioning from high school to higher education (particularly if community colleges are obliged to continue with remedial training as before);
- refresher training for previously unemployed or laid-off workers—the noncredit students; and
- raising the labor-force participation rate, as discussed in detail earlier.

The EIS results, model, and survey databases are very much *the* ingredients needed to navigate through this expanded role. There is therefore, as everyone in the community college world will agree, a need for alternative funding sources to fill in the gaps left behind from the shrinking traditional state funding sources even to support what's indicated in just the first bullet point. However, a lot more funding is needed on top of that to encompass the demands listed in the second and third bullet points as well. Courting alternative funding sources becomes an urgent priority.

The expanded use of the EIS results, as discussed throughout these pages, can help court alternative funding sources. Economic analysis of proposals based on the EIS, model, and survey databases provides much-appreciated information to private donors *in addition to why they donate money in the first place*. Donors have their own reasons for giving, and many are probably noneconomic. But if they know that their donations also contribute to the regional economic well-being, then the analysis should clearly provide a competitive edge in favor of the community colleges. In other words, the analysis may tip the scales toward funneling money the colleges' way.

It is all about the messaging: how to better tell the community college story and how the donors' money fits into that story.

Of course, college leaders should continue to make their case as usual to the state legislators, and to do so with more informative and improved messages that higher education is more deserving than other sectors, and explain why. Poorly communicating the investment analysis results makes it all the more difficult to convince taxpayers and their representatives—the legislators—that *not* funding the community colleges will be economically painful for the regions, even in bad economic times. This is the battle to get a bigger share of the shrinking pie from the taxpayers. But, to make up the loss of state support, the money has to come from somewhere else. So far, the solution has been to make up for the difference with higher tuition and fees. And *that* has its own set of problems.

The "how" of the long-term insurance policy, therefore, is improved economic messaging of the EIS results and what they mean for economic well-being of the region. Two outcomes will likely follow with success in raising funds for community colleges through alternative sources:

- Some financial relief through less reliance on state and federal funding, but all the while seeking to turn the tide on the continued erosion of these funding sources, or at least slow it down, and
- some enrollment relief through less reliance on offsetting public funding cuts with higher tuition and fees, but all the while keeping this option open if it makes economic sense.

These two bullet points require that college leaders become experts at communicating the economic benefits of supporting the community colleges. To do that, they need to fully understand the EIS results and what they mean. And they must be prepared to meet any political controversy both head-on and armed with credible data and analysis, not just anecdotes.

College leaders—the presidents in particular—must take the time to study and understand the economic underpinnings of the EIS results in order to improve the marketing message. The difference between the *broad* and *narrow* taxpayer investment perspectives discussed in chapter 3, for example, is a good place to start. This goes to the heart of the taxpayers' pocketbooks. In general, the colleges put far more money back into their state treasuries than they take out. The negative perception that the colleges are a drain on taxpayer funds is, in reality, the exact opposite. This also is a strong argument for conducting EISs annually, not just every three years or so. This will keep the colleges in the news and continuously inform and educate the stakeholders and the public about the important economic role of the colleges.

PRIVATE DONORS

Perhaps the broader title of this section should be *philanthropy*, defined in the Google dictionary as "the desire to promote the welfare of others, expressed especially by the generous donation of money to good causes." This is a vast and untapped source for community colleges. The year 2017 was a very good year for private giving across all sectors, in fact, it was the best year ever, totaling some $410 billion, divided as follows:[2]

- Individuals, 70 percent, $286 billion
- Foundations, 16 percent, $67 billion
- Bequest, 9 percent, $36 billion
- Corporate, 5 percent, $21 billion

Of that $410 billion total, only $59 billion, or 14.4 percent of the total, was given to higher education. Of that amount, 50 percent was given to 60 universities, which leaves roughly $30 billion. Of that amount, community colleges received only 6 percent, or $1.8 billion with the rest going to other universities. This works out to an average of approximately $1.4 million per public community college in the United States.

Let that sink in for a moment.

At the 2017 ACCT convention, there was a panel presentation led by Dr. Noah Brown, ACCT CEO, on the untapped potential of philanthropic giving in the United States. The bottom line at the end of that session was that community colleges have done a poor job in accessing this potential.

The reason why is probably that community colleges have for so long been dependent on the traditional sources and focused all of their efforts there. The fact that the annual battles with the state legislators are becoming incrementally more difficult each year does not trigger a revolt of sorts means that college presidents are still in their comfort zone—the difficulties are . . . well . . . only incremental. The prevailing sentiment is that continuing to court the traditional sources of funding is preferable to adding the burden of also becoming good at courting alternative sources of funding.

There is something fundamentally wrong with that sentiment. The good news is that *either/or* is not the question, *in addition to* is. More money is needed if the colleges are to expand their horizons as laid out in these pages, and that increase in the budgets is not likely to come from the state taxpayers. The best the colleges can hope for in focusing all efforts on state taxpayer funding is winning bigger slices of an incrementally smaller pie over time. By all means, those battles at the state level should still be fought, and fought well, but they should not be the only front where the colleges' efforts are expended. State funding of community colleges through appropriations and property taxes will remain the major sources for the foreseeable future, but they are not likely to increase over the long term. A second front must be opened—learning well how to approach private donors with winning strategies.

Our strong recommendation is that colleges focus their fund-raising efforts to at least triple their collections from the private donors—individuals, foundations, bequests, and corporations. A much-improved *economic* messaging will go a long way in this endeavor.

Angela White of Johnson Grassnickle Associates has a checklist of what college presidents should learn about how to best approach the private donors:[3]

> Know your donors' interests. Donors are becoming more and more educated and discerning about the causes they support, making the appeal more challenging. Your relationships with major gift donors remain extremely important, as individuals remain the largest source of giving to education. Nurture your relationships with donors and align your case for support with their motivations, emphasizing the significant impact of their philanthropic gifts.[4]

This first item on the checklist is to urge college leaders to intimately know the donors' interests and then formulate the soliciting message accordingly. When college leaders decide it is time to expand their fund-raising efforts, this is precisely what they will do. They are fully aware, of course, that the competition for donations is stiff, and so they will focus on becoming more educated and discerning about the market they are about to break into. As a result, their requests for increased support will become closely aligned with the donors' motivations to donate. The donor motivations, however, are all over the map, ranging from simply reducing their taxable income to endowing a chair in the arts. It will take some effort to do this, but aligning the requests with the donors' motivations requires some individual nurturing of potential donors.

Enter the EIS with a view to offering a competitive edge. The impact results may not necessarily be perfectly aligned with donors' motivations, but they do represent a dimension that may tip the scales. Donors will always recognize strong EIS results packaged in such a way as to complement their prime motivations as a very welcome addition. No donors dislike or disapprove of well-documented economic benefits that are generated from their donations. These benefits may not be their prime motivators for giving, but since they *can be* documented and made explicit in the college's solicitations, they will only add to, not detract from, the donors' prime motivations. They, therefore, provide an additional and quantitative dimension to why the donors give in the first place. The second item in the checklist is the following:

> Pay close attention to your online presence and outreach. Higher-education institutions experienced a 13.4 percent growth in online giving in 2017, continuing double-digit growth over the past three years. This continuous and substantial growth indicates that online giving has become an accepted and increasingly preferred method of giving to higher education; in fact, the institutions analyzed by the Blackbaud Index saw the greatest increase of any sector in 2017. Keeping abreast of innovative ways to use technology to reach, inform, and encourage donors to give will continue to be an important aspect of donor relationships.[5]

The online presence of the majority of community colleges is far from where it should be, to say the least. Despite the double-digit growth in online giving between 2014 and 2017, college websites are generally not inviting to potential donors, at least not in ways that facilitate donations. In fact, most college websites appear as if they were designed by committees, not with the end users in mind. To be a bit facetious, students and potential donors have to get through the college's smoking-on-campus policy before they get to what they are really looking for; at least that's what it seems like. The online presence should be improved to make it easier for potential donors to want to give to the college.

Uncluttering the websites for the students is another topic, and probably much bigger one, that needs to addressed in another book.

The top priority in improving the online presence is to locate subtle requests for donations on the homepage, in combination with, or in the context of, the EIS results. That context should be the summary of the results from the perspective of the region's citizens, both in terms of the impact the college has on the gross regional product (GRP), and the return on investment (ROI) from both the student and taxpayer perspectives.

A cleverly devised calculator should show that every state funding dollar the college loses over time translates to $X in potential GRP losses—the gains lost because of budgetary shortfalls—and that these losses could be prevented through private donations from individuals, foundations, bequests, or corporations. The *tenor* of that message should avoid lamenting a "woe-to-me" of the gradual losses of state funding over time; it should instead enthusiastically appeal to private donors to fill and exceed the funding gaps. The losses of state funding over time are opportunities for donors to step up their game and personalize the impacts that their donations have in economic terms. This would be an *added* incentive to their prime motivations for giving in the first place, whatever they may be. The third item on the checklist is the following:

> Stay abreast of changing tax legislation. Being informed about adjustments to tax laws is increasingly important in the current climate of change, and donors will appreciate your help in navigating this landscape. No one can predict the impact of the 2017 legislation or any upcoming changes but working closely with donors who may want to adjust their giving priorities will be important.[6]

Tax legislation, of course, is very much correlated with private donations. When tax exemptions are reduced or removed, donations to the colleges will most certainly fall. The reduction of personal or corporate taxes is a prime motivator for giving for most donors. In the context of taxes, the message drawn from the EIS should only complement the impact of any changes in the tax legislation on donations. On one hand, the message derived from the EIS should describe what donations will do for the region and its taxpayers—an appealing message to any donor. On the other hand, the tax legislation clarifies what the donors will save on their tax bills for this year as a result of their donations—also an appealing message to any donor. The above-mentioned calculator could be designed to show the amounts saved on taxes on donations of a given size.

As this item on the checklist states, no one can predict the impact on donations as a result of changes in tax legislation, and any help in navigating this landscape can only have positive upsides—there are no downsides.

The fourth item on the checklist is about donor-advised funds. "A donor-advised fund, or DAF, is a giving vehicle established as a public charity. It allows donors to make a charitable contribution, receive an immediate tax deduction and then recommend grants from the fund over time."[7]

> Connect with donor-advised fund (DAF) donors. Donor-advised funds are one of the fastest-growing giving vehicles in the U.S., and the education sector receives more grants from DAFs than any other sector. As more donors choose to give this way, transparency is becoming more important for nonprofit organizations, as donor-advised funds research each organization prior to granting funds. But keep in mind that the ultimate giving decisions are still up to the individual donor, which confirms the continuing importance of those relationships.[8]

Use of a DAF is a central feature that should be prominent in the colleges' online presence. It could range from a simple guide to the DAFs available, to a more detailed description of what a DAF is and how it helps navigate the complicated landscape of the impact of private donations on both the donors and the region affected. The dots between the implications of new and old tax legislation, the regional economic benefits of the donations (drawn from the EIS), regardless of the prime motivation for why donors donate, and the DAFs should be connected to complete the online presence. The potential for the bigger donations from private individuals, bequests, and corporations, however, needs a lot more individual attention from the college presidents.

In the end, the combination of a highly visible and functional online presence for potential donors, plus an aggressive focus on approaching larger donors individually should, all else being equal, lead to a much larger market share of donations in the higher-education space. Instead of the current 6 percent market share or approximately a calculated average of $1.4 million per community college, perhaps a more aggressive focus on courting alternative funding sources will, and let's dream just a little, perhaps triple that market share—to an average of $4.2 million per college. Such an increase will go a long way in successfully addressing some of the issues discussed in earlier chapters of this book.

CONCLUSION

The need to begin in earnest to court alternative sources of funding for community colleges is a wake-up call. The colleges' market share of donations from private individuals, foundations, bequests, and corporations is woefully small. And this clearly tells the story that community colleges have for far too long depended almost solely on the availability of public funding for their budgets.

This wake-up call is intended to shake the colleges out of their slumber of not recognizing the incremental decrease in the availability of public funding of community colleges and increased competition from other sectors. Some colleges have been clever, and some years they manage to secure a relatively bigger slice of a slowly decreasing funding base. But the handwriting is on the wall, and the probability of the occurrence of years like that is slowly decreasing as well. The public funding prospects for community colleges *under the current system* will remain bleak for the foreseeable future.

So, the colleges must look elsewhere for supplemental funding if they wish to continue their role as significant economic players in their respective regions. This, however, means that college leaders must acquire new skills—skills in effectively approaching the large private philanthropic donor market to increase their current dismal market share of only 6 percent of $30 billion donated to the higher-education sector. The easiest part of those acquired skills is to vastly improve the online presence of the colleges' websites to help unclutter the process of giving for potential donors. Uncluttering means that donors are helped to navigate the landscape of:

- why to give (the donors' prime motivations),

- how to give (in-kind or dollars),
- through which vehicle (DAFs or others),
- the tax implications (savings) for them (the donation calculator), and
- the regional economic benefits as a result of the donations (by adapting the EIS results for that purpose—also the donation calculator).

The skill the colleges need to acquire in this space is how to effectively approach the larger individual donors, foundations, or corporations. They need individual attention in the forms of invitations to meetings, seats on advisory boards, presentations of college visions along with funding needs, explanations of the EIS results and the extent to which they will be increased by the donations contemplated, and detailed explanations of the personal tax advantages of the donations.

NOTES

1. Michael Mitchell, M. Leachman, K. Masterson, and S. Waxman, *Unkept Promises: State Cuts to Higher Education Threaten Access and Equity* (Washington, DC: Center on Budget and Policy Priorities, October 4, 2018).

2. Giving USA, "Americans Gave $410.02 Billion to Charity in 2017, Crossing the $400 Billion Mark for the First Time," GivingUSA.org, June 13, 2018, https://givingusa.org/giving-usa-2018-americans-gave-410-02-billion-to-charity-in-2017-crossing-the-400-billion-mark-for-the-first-time/.

3. Angela White, "Giving USA 2018: Implications for Higher Ed," Johnson Grassnickle Associates, July 20, 2018, http://info.jgacounsel.com/blog/giving-usa-2018-implications-for-higher-ed.

4. Ibid.
5. Ibid.
6. Ibid.

7. National Philanthropic Trust, "What Is a Donor-Advised Fund (DAF)?" https://www.nptrust.org/what-is-a-donor-advised-fund/.

8. Ibid.

9

CONCLUSIONS AND MESSAGES TO COLLEGE PRESIDENTS

SETTING THE STAGE

What are we to make of all this? What should college presidents do once they have the economic impact study (EIS) results? Is the EIS something to do every two or three years, or should it be an annual undertaking? The answers to these questions are sprinkled throughout these pages, so here we only want to summarize and conclude. The short answers are:

- take the time to understand what the EIS results mean—learn the underpinnings of the EIS, particularly the differences between gross and net impacts.
- let the EIS enrich proposed changes—know the next steps after completion of the EIS, including "what-if" analyses and what they may bring to the table in terms of future funding prospects.

All community colleges have summary statements of the presidents' duties as chief executive officers. First and foremost, the president acts as the executive officer of the Board of Governors—or trustees. The board, therefore, is the actual boss, and the president's role is to implement the decisions made. All these decisions, of course, are framed in the context of the college's master plan, which is a lofty expression of goals and objectives and specific targets. So, the president should not be alone; there are several internal-to-the-college stakeholders that must be on the same page.

But they aren't. Sometimes, the culture of a college is such that the president assumes the lead and the board rubber-stamps his or her leadership. Sometimes, probably more often, it is the other way around. The political climate in the region where the college is located always dictates the intensity of friction or tension between the president and the board over many issues. In most cases, business is conducted in an orderly fashion, but for many colleges there is unrest. There will always be rough waters to navigate because no college president can please all constituencies all the time. There will be winners and losers and the losers tend to become the more vocal of the two.

So, given the potential for turmoil in the upper echelons of a college leadership and the high stress quotient that comes with the job of president, how does an EIS fit in? Does it exacerbate the problems, or solve them? Does it ease the process of getting everyone on the same page, or does it add to the tension?

The easy answers first—it exacerbates the problems for the president if the EIS results are perceived to be low—like when they choose to compare them to a neighboring college—even though they are still above threshold levels. (They should *not* compare the results to those of other colleges, although most do anyway.) And, it exacerbates the problems when the EIS is perceived as just one more thing added to the daily management burden of the president. As we have often seen, the administration must now deal with an entirely new layer of potential problems, such as the institutional research office may lament the added burden of having to collect the college data for the study in addition to an already overloaded work schedule. Moreover, and probably more often than not, the economics department at the college complains that *they* weren't asked to conduct the study. There are all sorts of arguments mounted when an EIS is proposed because it may, just may . . . upset the status quo, or the comfortable equilibrium the faculty and staff have found themselves in. After all, a study like this may lead to the second phase—a "what-if" analysis of program changes—and *that* may question the validity of certain programs, which could potentially upset well-established fiefdoms.

Now for the more complicated answer, the EIS also solves problems when the results are high, or higher than neighboring colleges. Again,

CONCLUSIONS AND MESSAGES TO COLLEGE PRESIDENTS

they will compare the results, and someone will come out on top. For those who do compare, the results will add comfort, even though comparisons are wrong, as discussed in earlier chapters. The EIS is not a panacea. It has the *potential* to at least partially deal with other issues, and it is that potential that we want colleges to realize. The EIS is not a necessary evil. It is a tool, a starting point, or focal point that can make everything clearer. Our objective is for college presidents to recognize it as such and use the methodology and results to at least partially resolve some of the issues. In other words, our aim is to move beyond categorizing the EIS as a "nice-to-have" to a power tool used to address the bigger issues such as loan default rates, low completion rates, and so on.

A small subset of college presidents, however, probably view the EIS as a necessary evil. They reluctantly participate if the state leaders agree to conduct a statewide study wherein all colleges would have to participate. These presidents may have had a political fallout experience with an EIS conducted in the past and are understandably reluctant to repeat the experience. Besides, they are probably not trained economists and may be less interested in how their colleges perform in the economic arena and more interested in measuring performance relative to the master plans without having to count the dollars and cents. Often, they believe the stakeholders are no different since most of them are not economists either. These colleges operate without having the regional economic well-being high on their list of priorities. Yet, when they *do* participate in a statewide EIS, their results still tend to exceed the threshold values, and so the study is "nice to have" but not perceived as necessary.

A larger subset of college presidents understands that the EIS is periodically necessary but do not fully understand the results in terms of their potential use. They are the ones who check the box of having conducted an EIS, say every three years, and then move on to other things. They rarely capitalize on the *potential* use of the methodology and results, and they advocate on behalf of their colleges, not the taxpayers. They are not particularly familiar with the regional economic base, its workforce and demographics, and have not assumed an active leadership role in the region's economic development. Probably, most colleges are in this category.

A third category of college presidents, again a small subset, are those who take the EIS results and do with them precisely as we have recommended in these pages. They address other issues leveraging the EIS results, using the EIS results to promote their colleges in ways that go far beyond the magnitudes of the results themselves, and they actively lobby for parents not to send their children *elsewhere* for an education, because that is effectively sending money out of the regional economy. They are economic development leaders in their regional communities and they act on behalf of the taxpayers, not just the college.

It is this third subset of college presidents we wish to increase in numbers. These are the ones who get it, who sit up and take notice, and the ones whose actions as presidents reach beyond the boundaries of the college and into the economic well-being of the regions they serve. They are also the ones who do not call just one press conference to announce the results, but use them in innovative ways on every occasion. There are several college presidents who comes close to this ideal, but three stand out. One is Dr. Steve VanAusdle, now former president of Walla Walla Community College in Washington State, and a 2013 winner of the Aspen Prize for Community College Excellence. The second is Dr. Larry Keen of Fayetteville Technical and Community College in North Carolina. The third is Dr. Anne Kress of Monroe Community College in New York. These college presidents have milked the EIS results in far more innovative ways than we ever thought possible. They are economic development leaders in their communities, and the colleges have stellar reputations as dominant regional economic players.

To move many more college presidents from the second to the third subset is the goal. And it is probably ambitious because it needs to happen sooner rather than later. To emulate the college presidents who are already in this subset requires an entirely different way of thinking (outside the box, as the saying goes) about the issues in general. *All* issues can be expressed in economic terms. The (worrisome) accreditation meetings are coming up next month; the student-loan default rate is hovering in dangerous territory; the union is signaling aggressive salary negotiations to begin two months from now; and the mix of programs offered has been loudly targeted by some local residents as irrelevant. So much to worry about, so little time, and the money available to address these and other issues is becoming increasingly scarce. Many

CONCLUSIONS AND MESSAGES TO COLLEGE PRESIDENTS

college presidents run full-steam and are registering high readings on the stress scale.

Colleges have master plans, however defined, and progress must be demonstrated. To treat all issues as economic problems will only reduce the confusion that is typically associated with a dominant management style of putting out fires as they occur.

TAKE THE TIME TO UNDERSTAND WHAT THE RESULTS MEAN

We began the discussion in this book with a distinction between the two main components of the EIS: the regional and investment components. The regional analysis is what any EIS will include. It is simply a measure of how much of the region's gross regional product (GRP) the college can explain, or account for. It is, therefore, a measure of the importance of the college as an economic player in the region it serves, relative to all of the other players.

Pay particular attention to the word "impact." Do the results mean what they say? A three-county region, for example, may have a GRP of $10 billion, of which the college explains 5 percent, or $500 million. That's the measured impact. What does this mean? Is this a *good and strong* number, or is it weak or relatively insignificant? This can be answered only by looking at your 5 percent relative to the impact from the collection of other industries and companies that claim an impact on the size of the GRP, up to the sum total of 100 percent. Can any of these other industries claim an impact even close to your 5 percent?

Five percent is 5 percent—that number doesn't tell much by itself. It needs context. And that context is twofold.

First, an impact measure is a *net* number, not a *gross* number. It reflects what the regional economy would have looked like without the college in its midst. That means that only outside-the-region money used to fund the college is counted. There are lots of counterfactuals—adjustments to the college funding—to account for to arrive at the net impact measure. Were it not for the presence of the college in that region, outside federal money or state appropriations would not have flowed in. Only *new* money flowing into the region *because the college is there* is counted. As that new money is spent, it generates a multiplier effect, which is part of the $500 million, or 5 percent of the GRP measure.

Second, to give meaning to the $500 million impact, it should be compared to other economic players in the region. Here is the reality. Few of the other players, if any, could *individually* lay claim to as much as 5 percent of the total GRP, or whatever the college can claim as its impact. The college presidents need to fully understand this. Furthermore, they need to understand what the 5 percent is made up of, then be able to communicate this to the community stakeholders with confidence, being prepared to respond when others try to poke holes in the arguments made.[1]

The reason why other companies and industries have difficulties comparing well to the economic prowess of the college is attributable to one fact alone—the alumni effect, or what we call the productivity effect. This is the cumulative impact of the college having been in business for decades educating students who subsequently enter the regional workforce and add to the economic value of that region each year. There is a large difference between the *products* of colleges and the *products* of local businesses. The former is education and *its* value does not dissipate after just one year. It is like the Energizer bunny: it keeps on adding value for as long as the students, now employees (or owners) of regional companies, remain in the workforce. The education they received at the community college at some point in time still has value. Over time, this builds both the quantity and the quality—the productivity—of the regional workforce, which adds cumulatively to the economic value of the college over time.

The latter—a productivity effect—cannot be claimed by other local industries or companies in the region. The values of *their* products—the widgets they produce—are unlike the value of education; they dissipate once they are produced and sold. In fact, the very presence of these industries inside the region is, at least partially, attributable to the college providing them with a decent and capable workforce. This is the agglomeration effect that also illustrates the economic importance of the presence of the community college in the region. A well-qualified workforce now and the assurance that the supply of equally well-qualified workers will continue unabated into the future are powerful attractants for companies.

The investment analysis from the perspectives of the students and the taxpayers is different—it does not measure impacts. It is not a component of the impact measure of the GRP with and without the college. Instead, it adds needed *context* to the GRP impact measure. For students, it answers the question of whether it makes economic sense for them to attend the college. If it doesn't, the college has a problem. Pretty soon the students will find out that attending college is not a paying proposition for them, so they will no longer enroll. For the taxpayers, it answers the question of whether it makes economic sense to fund the colleges. If it doesn't, the college has a problem here as well, because eventually the taxpayers will wake up to the fact that they are pouring money into a black hole. It all depends on the threshold levels. The students wake up to returns on investment (ROIs) below the threshold levels faster than the taxpayers and legislators. For the students, the ROI is up front and personal—it is felt. For the taxpayers and legislators, the ROI is not personal nor acutely felt.

The student and taxpayer ROIs are simply benchmark measures. If they exceed threshold values, then we have the luxury of breathing room to experiment, doing things differently next year, but always with a view to move the needle toward improving the impact results. Of course, we want the student and taxpayer ROIs—the investment analysis results—to always be higher, but that can be tricky. The ROI does not take into account the efficacy of the *college's* spending, but it does account for the profile of the student body, which changes from one year to the next. That profile is not only characterized by the demographics, it is also characterized by the employment patterns of the students while enrolled. And that affects the opportunity cost—the most significant cost incurred by the students for their education. The opportunity cost is also affected by the economic cycle, which changes from one year to the next. In good economic times, the employment opportunities are plentiful, and the opportunity cost for students tends to be lower because more of them are gainfully employed while attending. This generally translates into higher student ROIs. But, in good economic times, enrollment also takes a dip—fewer students are attending. So, for a smaller student body the ROIs may be higher (an improvement), but the college's impact on GRP may be comparatively lower because the student body may have shrunk. In bad economic times, the reverse holds.

The college presidents need to fully understand these dynamics and make them second nature. Complex questions arise, and the presidents should be able to answer them with confidence. Ideally, the goal should be that the college is perceived by the stakeholders as a significant part of the regional economic development mosaic, with the college president as its leader. That's the ideal. And so, when explanations are demanded as to why the impact results are different between years, which they always are, the college presidents should not be stymied for lack of knowledge of the reasons.

Beginning with confidence in the model used to generate the impact results, they should intuitively know that comparing results between years should be avoided because so many interdependent variables not under their control change. Business cycles come and go, and the regional data will change significantly from one year to the next. And so will the college data, the student numbers and their profiles, and the budgets. When mixing an entirely different regional data set this year with a completely different data set from the college, the results *will* be different from those obtained when the last EIS was conducted.

Likewise, comparisons of results *between* colleges should also be avoided because it would be comparing apples to oranges. Each college offers unique programs of study, they are located in regions that may be either economically depressed or thriving, and they serve entirely different student bodies. All of this should be second nature to the college presidents, and they should not be taken by surprise by any economic development question as it relates to the education offered by the college.

LET THE EIS ENRICH YOUR PROPOSED SOLUTIONS TO DIFFERENT PROBLEMS

Suppose a college president names 10 prominent issues he or she must address during the year, with many of them at risk of political fallout if not addressed right away. It is like walking a tightrope where any misstep could prove calamitous. (Come to think of it, this may be a main reason why there is such a high turnover among community college presidents.) Many college presidents, if not most of them, of course address the issues as they appear on the horizon. They are putting out

CONCLUSIONS AND MESSAGES TO COLLEGE PRESIDENTS

small and big fires. They don't know when an issue becomes widely exposed in the media and so reacting to it becomes urgent so as to placate any specific accusations, deserved or not. It should be said in this context, however, that college presidents who are recognized as leaders in safeguarding the regional economic well-being are in a much better position to calm things down any time there is political turmoil.

We have been singling out some of the issues in these pages and have suggested dealing with them by leveraging the EIS results. Issues like the default rate on student loans, low graduation rates, and the imbalance between supply and demand for specific workforce skills can, at least partially, be addressed through the EIS mechanism by using the model and the databases to simulate the impacts of proposed changes. If we do A to address issue B, then the resulting economic impact will be C.

If the issue is low graduation rates, we can use EIS data to highlight the importance of the *noncredit* side of the services provided by the college, the high number of students who are nondegree seeking. These services add tremendous economic value in the workforce after the students have received their up-skilling. This, of course, offsets the value of the credentials forgone. If the problem is a high default rate on student loans of the kind that brings the college into dangerous territory on federal funding eligibility, the EIS can be used to provide strong arguments in favor of tweaking programs to be much more responsive to the regional workforce needs. Higher earnings are the result, and *that* increases the ability to repay loans.

Dealing with other issues using the EIS mechanism, of course, is not seamless or an overly easy task. The college, however, has a significant head start. An EIS in hand means that the college now has access to the following:

The EIS analysts—the contractor who has access to the most recent databases on the region (the regional economic base, demographics, workforce employment and earnings numbers).

The college database—compiled by the college institutional researchers.

The model through the EIS analysts—the mechanisms through which the different "what-if" scenarios can be simulated.

Regional and investment analysis results—for one locked-in snapshot scenario consisting of the student body numbers and profile, student achievements, budget and sources of revenues, and program mix.

Without the EIS, the budget request process will likely consist of doing more of the same next year, with perhaps a proposed cost-of-living increase tacked on. If there are any new proposed initiatives on the horizon, such as changes in the programs mix (tweaking or dropping some programs or adding some new ones), they will be proposed without any regional economic well-being context or analyses that demonstrate the economic feasibility of the initiatives. There will be no reference made to any strategy to move closer to the production possibilities frontier. The budget requests will likely be made in the context of what the college needs to operate, and not with any reference to the college's role in the overall regional economic well-being.

A college demonstrating with analyses and measures of the extent to which the regional taxpayers gain will succeed in getting the budget it requests much more so than the college that doesn't.

NOTE

1. When asked by one client to make comparisons of the college's annual impact to that of the perceived main industry of the state as represented by its association, the comparison reflected well on the college. It reflected less well on the main industry, because the college's impact was actually the same, and it was *public perception* that that particular industry (in this case, represented by an association) was the dominant economic driver for the state. Everybody would mention this particular industry when asked about the state's economy (like the auto industry in Michigan); virtually no one would think of naming the college. So, in the interest of safeguarding this perception, the association in this case made a *political* argument to discourage such a revealing message to be spread. But a college president will also gain some bounce in his or her steps by knowing the reality that the college is not subservient to an industry now perceived to be number one in economic importance for the state. There are lots of arrows in the quiver to still have plenty of successes in a regional context when communicating it in special settings, such as speeches to the Rotarians and Kiwanis, economic development forums, community meetings, and the like.

BIBLIOGRAPHY

Amadeo, Kimberly. 2019. "US Manufacturing, Statistics and Outlook." *The Balance*, January 5. https://www.thebalance.com/u-s-manufacturing-what-it-is-statistics-and-outlook-3305575.

Anderson, Tom. 2017. "More Than 1.1 Million Borrowers Defaulted on Their Federal Student Loans Last Year." CNBC Personal Finance, March 14. https://www.cnbc.com/2017/03/14/more-than-11-million-borrowers-defaulted-on-their-federal-student-loans-last-year.html.

Aspen Institute. 2019. *College Excellence Program: Selection Process.* https://highered.aspeninstitute.org/aspen-prize-program/selection-process/#.

Becker, Gary S. 1993. *Human Capital: A Theoretical and Empirical Analysis, with Special Reference to Education.* New York: Columbia College Press for NBER.

Binkley, Collin. 2018. "DeVos Warns of Crisis Amid Ballooning Student Debt." Associated Press, November 27. https://www.apnews.com/383f53f0cbb2439792f9ffcd06ce196e.

Caplan, Bryan Douglas. 2018. *The Case Against Education.* Princeton, NJ, and Oxford: Princeton University Press.

Carnevale, Anthony P., Jeff Strohl, and Neil Ridley. 2017. *Good Jobs That Pay without a BA: A State-by-State Analysis.* Georgetown University, Center on Education and the Workforce, McCourt School of Public Policy.

Center on Budget and Policy Priorities. 2017. "Policy Basics: Where Do Our Tax Dollars Go?" cbpp.org, April 24. https://www.cbpp.org/research/state-budget-and-tax/policy-basics-where-do-our-state-tax-dollars-go.

Chen, Grace. 2017. "Studies Show Community College May Offer Superior ROI to Some Four-Year Schools." *Community College Review*, September 4. https://www.communitycollegereview.com/blog/studies-show-community-college-may-offer-superior-roi-to-some-four-year-schools.

Christophersen, Kjell A., Tim Nadreau, and Aaron Olanie. 2014. "The Rights and Wrongs of Economic Impact Analysis for Colleges and Universities." Emsi blog, January 7.

CNBC. 2019. "Free College Is Now a Reality in Nearly 20 States." cnbc.com, March 18. https://www.cnbc.com/2019/03/12/free-college-now-a-reality-in-these-states.html.

Consumer Federation of America.2017. "More Than 1 Million Federal Student Loan Defaults in 2016." Press release, March 14.https://consumerfed.org/press_release/new-data-1-1-million-federal-student-loan-defaults-2016/.

Delisle, Jason D. 2018. "The Left Gives Community Colleges Another Free Pass for Unpaid Student Loans." AEI, August 29. http://www.aei.org/publication/the-left-gives-community-colleges-another-free-pass-for-unpaid-student-loans/.

Douglas-Gabriel, Danielle. 2016. "Remedial Classes Have Become a Hidden Cost of College." *Washington Post*, April 6. https://www.washingtonpost.com/news/grade-point/wp/2016/04/06/remedial-classes-have-become-a-hidden-cost-of-college/?noredirect=on&utm_term=. edd9de2f2bb7.
Economic Modeling Specialists International. 2014. *Demonstrating the Value of America's Community Colleges, Analysis of the Economic Impact and Return on Investment of Education.*
Education Corner. 2019. *Community Colleges vs. Universities.* https://www.educationcorner.com/community-college-vs-university.html.
Giving USA. 2018. "Americans Gave $410.02 Billion to Charity in 2017, Crossing the $400 Billion Mark for the First Time." GivingUSA.org, June 13. https://givingusa.org/giving-usa-2018-americans-gave-410-02-billion-to-charity-in-2017-crossing-the-400-billion-mark-for-the-first-time/.
Henderson, David. 2008. "A Pareto-Optimal Move." Econlib.org. EconLog, October 27.
Hudson, David. 2015. "The President Proposes to Make Community College Free for Responsible Students for 2 Years," The White House, January 18. https://obamawhitehouse.archives.gov/blog/2015/01/08/president-proposes-make-community-college-free-responsible-students-2-years.
Jaeger, David, and Marianne Page. 1996. "Degrees Matter: New Evidence on Sheepskin Effects in the Returns to Education." *Review of Economics and Statistics* 78 (4): 733–40.
Kahlenberg, Richard D. 2015. "How Higher Education Funding Shortchanges Community Colleges." The Century Foundation, May 28. https://tcf.org/content/report/how-higher-education-funding-shortchanges-community-colleges/?agreed=1.
Kreighbaum, Andrew. 2018. "GAO: Colleges, Consultants Game Rules to Lower Default Rates." *Inside Higher Ed*, April 27. https://www.insidehighered.com/news/2018/04/27/gao-finds-colleges-manipulating-loan-default-rates-keep-access-federal-aid.
Leigh, Andrew, and Chris Ryan. 2008. "Estimating Returns to Education Using Different Natural Experiments Techniques." *Economics of Education Review* 27:149–60.
Luebke, Bob. 2016. "Why Free College Tuition Is a Bad Idea." Civitas Institute, February 4. https://www.nccivitas.org/2016/16909/.
Marcus, Jon. 2016. "Colleges Confront the Simple Math That Keeps Students from Graduation on Time." *The Hechinger Report*, February 17. https://hechingerreport.org/colleges-confront-the-simple-math-that-keeps-students-from-graduating-on-time/.
Megan, Kenneth, Shai Akabas, and Jake Varn. 2017. *Higher Education Trends: Rising Costs, Stagnant Outcomes, State Initiatives.* Washington, DC: Bipartisan Policy Center. https://bipartisanpolicy.org/wp-content/uploads/2019/03/BPC-Higher-Education-Rising-Costs-Stagnant-Outcomes.pdf.
Mincer, Jacob. 1958. "Investment in Human Capital and Personal Income Distribution." *Journal of Political Economy* 66 (4): 281–302.
———. 1974. *Schooling, Experience and Earnings.* New York: National Bureau of Economic Research.
Mitchell, Michael, M. Leachman, K. Masterson, and S. Waxman. 2018. "Unkept Promises: State Cuts to Higher Education Threaten Access and Equity." Center on Budget and Policy Priorities, October 4. https://www.cbpp.org/research/state-budget-and-tax/unkept-promises-state-cuts-to-higher-education-threaten-access-and.
Molitor, Christopher J. 2003. *Price Elasticity of Demand for Community Colleges.* Report prepared for CCbenefits.
Molitor, Chris, and Duane Leigh. 2001. *Estimating the Returns to Schooling: Calculating the Difference Between Causation and Correlation.* Report prepared for CCbenefits, Inc.
National Philanthropic Trust. n.d. "What Is a Donor-Advised Fund (DAF)?" https://www.nptrust.org/what-is-a-donor-advised-fund/.
O'Banion, Terry. 2013. *Access, Success, and Completion: A Primer for Community College Faculty, Administrators, Staff, and Trustees.* Chandler, AZ: League for Innovation in the Community College.

Office of Management and Budget. "Circular A-94 Appendix C: Real Interest Rates on Treasury Notes and Bonds of Specified Maturities (in Percent)." Last modified November 2016. https://obamawhitehouse.archives.gov/omb/circulars_a094/a94_appx-c.

Reinhart, Carmen, and Kenneth Rogoff. 2011. *This Time Is Different: Eight Centuries of Financial Folly*. Princeton, NJ: Princeton University Press.

Ross, Janell. 2014. "Is Open-Access Community College a Bad Idea?" *The Atlantic*, June 23. https://www.theatlantic.com/politics/archive/2014/06/is-open-access-community-college-a-bad-idea/431052/.

Siegfried, John J., Allen R. Sanderson, and Peter McHenry. 2006. "The Economic Impact of Colleges and Universities." Working Paper No. 6-W12. Department of Economics, Vanderbilt University.

Trading Economics. 2019. "United States Labor Force Participation Rate." https://tradingeconomics.com/united-states/labor-force-participation-rate.

US Department of Labor. 2019. Bureau of Labor Statistics website. "Labor Force Statistics." bls.gov, January 15.

US Department of the Treasury. 1998. *The Economic Costs of Smoking in the United States and the Benefits of Comprehensive Tobacco Legislation*. Office of Public Affairs Report-3113. http://www.treasury.gov/press-center/press-releases/Documents/tobacco.pdf.

Watson, Philip, Joshua Wilson, Dawn Thilmany, and Susan Winter. 2007. "Determining Economic Contributions and Impacts: What Is the Difference and Why Do We Care?" *Journal of Regional Analysis and Policy* 37 (2): 1–15.

White, Angela. 2018. "Giving USA 2018: Implications for Higher Ed." Johnson Grassnickle Associates, July 20. http://info.jgacounsel.com/blog/giving-usa-2018-implications-for-higher-ed2018.

Willis, R. J. 2001. *Handbook of Labor Economics*, vol. 1. Amsterdam: North-Holland Press.

Woodhouse, Kelly. 2015. "Closures to Triple." *Inside Higher Ed*, September 28. https://www.insidehighered.com/news/2015/09/28/moodys-predicts-college-closures-triple-2017.

ABOUT THE AUTHOR

Kjell Christophersen is a senior economist with 40 years of international and domestic experience. He is the cofounder and recently retired senior economist of Economic Modeling Specialists International—Emsi—a company specializing in economic impact analysis, labor market/workforce development forecasting, and economic growth analysis. His work with community colleges began in 2000 with a consulting contract with ACCT to develop the first version of the economic model measuring the impact a community college has on the region it serves. This effort blossomed into the company Emsi, headquartered in Moscow, Idaho, with offices in the UK and Dallas, Texas.

Dr. Christophersen also has extensive international experience in Africa, the Middle East, Asia, Europe, and the Caribbean as an economic development consultant, both long and short term, working for clients such as USAID and the World Bank. He has worked in nearly 70 countries and served as team leader on projects involving economic modeling; project designs and evaluations; natural resource management assessments; planning, feasibility, and recurrent cost studies; training needs assessments; training in economic and financial analysis; the economics of ecotourism; and environmental assessments from an economics perspective. Before Emsi, Dr. Christophersen was a senior manager for the International Resources Group (1983–2001), associate professor at the University of Idaho (1977–1983), and an adjunct associate professor at Washington State University (1992–1998). He is fluent in English and Norwegian and nearly fluent in French.

www.ingramcontent.com/pod-product-compliance
Lightning Source LLC
Chambersburg PA
CBHW030137240426
43672CB00005B/159